the fruit of all my grief

the fruit of all my grief

Lives in the Shadows
of the American Dream

J. MALCOLM GARCIA

Seven Stories Press

New York • Oakland • London

Seven Stories Press
140 Watts Street
New York, NY 10013
www.sevenstories.com

Library of Congress Cataloging-in-Publication Data

Names: Garcia, J. Malcolm, 1957- author.
Title: The fruit of all my grief : lives in the shadows of the American
    dream / J. Malcolm Garcia.
Description: New York : Seven Stories Press, [2019]
Identifiers: LCCN 2019017120 | ISBN 9781609809539 (paperback) | ISBN
    9781609809546 (ebook)
Subjects: LCSH: Social problems--United States. | Marginality,
    Social--United States. | American Dream. | United States--Social
    conditions--21st century.
Classification: LCC HN59.2 .G35 2019 | DDC 306.0973--dc23
LC record available at https://lccn.loc.gov/2019017120

9 8 7 6 5 4 3 2 1

College professors and high school and middle school teachers may order free examination copies of Seven Stories Press titles. To order, visit www.sevenstories.com, or
fax on school letterhead to (212) 226-1411.

. . .

These stories appeared, some in different versions, in *Guernica: A Magazine of Arts & Politics* ("Fishing with the King," November 2010; "The Life Sentence of Dicky Joe Jackson and His Family," April 2014; "Sanctuary," March 2017); *The Massachusetts Review* ("Nothing Went to Waste: Considering the Life of Ben Kennedy," Summer 2012); *McSweeney's* ("What Happens After Sixteen Years in Prison?," January 2013); *Oxford American* ("Smoke Signals," Summer 2011; "New Missions," Spring 2012; and "Backyard Battlefields," Summer 2012); *River Teeth* ("And the Walls Came Tumbling Down," Fall 2012); *Virginia Quarterly Review* ("A Product of This Town," January 2008); and *The Best American Nonrequired Reading 2009* ("We Are Not Just Refugees," Summer 2009).

Take from my hand
Put in your hands
The fruit of all my grief
—Alabama Shakes

My eyes often open when I see a limping person
   going down the street.
That person's wrestled with God, I think.
—William Goyen

Contents

Preface

The first story in this collection, "Sanctuary," came about as I followed news accounts of President Trump's initial crackdown on undocumented people in 2017. I contacted organizations that worked with immigrants and learned about a Mexican man, Sixto Paz, who had taken refuge in a Phoenix, Arizona, church for almost a year. I wondered, Who is this guy and others like him? Beyond the one or two quotes attributed to them in news stories, who are they, really? What are their dreams, ambitions, their disappointments? They are statistics. What else are they? What is our breathless, twenty-four-hour news cycle missing about them? I had to find out. I contacted the church and arranged to meet Sixto.

I often find my stories through the news and in chance encounters. In 2005, I was reporting from Port-au-Prince, Haiti, when I met a man by the name of Michael from Texas who housed homeless teenage boys. We spent no more than an hour together, if that. Five years later, after a catastrophic earthquake struck Haiti and killed thousands of people, I thought of Michael and wondered if he and the boys he sheltered survived. I tracked Michael down and then flew to Port-au-Prince and spent ten days with him as he tried to rebuild his shelter, his life, and the lives of the children he cared for.

Sixto, Michael, and the others profiled in this collection survived their ordeals. Their struggles changed and defined them, as do our own. They give meaning to our lives. They are our history and often reflect the times in which we live. They are worth telling and retelling and remembering.

The lives lurking beneath the surface of the everyday continue to intrigue me. My initial judgment of someone I don't know, based on the slimmest of information—their appearance, the sound of their voice, their expressions—does not satisfy.

We will continue to make assumptions about strangers through the impressions made by the briefest of encounters. No matter how flawed those conclusions, no matter how different we may think we are from them, most of us share a common routine. We get up each morning. We make it through each day. We sleep at night and ready ourselves for the next day without knowing what it may hold, what challenges we'll have to surmount, and how others will judge us.

We persevere.

—J. Malcolm Garcia
San Diego, February 2019

Sanctuary

Sixto Paz opens a door and shows me the music room. He sleeps on a bed across from a piano, sheets neatly tucked, a rack of clothes on hangers beside it. Shelves of books. A whiteboard. A table, some chairs, and a well-thumbed Bible open to the Book of Genesis. Sixto crashes out at about midnight and wakes up at four. He has trouble sleeping.

His last night in his Lexington Avenue place. Well . . . he hadn't *known* it was his last night at home in Phoenix. He knew he might have to leave, adapt to something not his home, to this church, but when? He had tried not to think about it. Leave family, leave work, leave his life, and come here and do nothing but wait for people he did not know to decide his fate. No, he would put that thought off as long as he could.

Sixto is forty-eight. He moved to the States from Mexico at the same time the Reagan administration's 1986 immigration law passed Congress. Among other things, the law admitted undocumented laborers for temporary and in some cases permanent residence. Sixto worked and traveled freely and legally in and out of the country. For more than twenty-five years, he built a life in Phoenix. He fathered a family, two daughters and a son, all U.S. citizens. He has no criminal record. But in 2002 the Department of Homeland Security refused to renew his work permit, which had given him authorization to work as a "nonimmigrant." Sixto blames the decision on changing immigration laws fueled by a populist backlash that accused immigrants of taking jobs from American citizens.

Seven years later, in 2009, he was stopped at a checkpoint near Yuma, Arizona. He was charged with remaining in the United States longer than his work permit allowed and held at a service processing center near Phoenix. He spent the next seven years fighting deportation in court. His attorney, Jose Peñalosa, told me that he always knew the court might rule against Sixto. He had heard that Shadow Rock United Church of Christ in North Phoenix offered sanctuary to undocumented migrants. Federal immigration and border authorities in most cases avoid detaining people who are staying in churches, schools, and hospitals—"sensitive locations," according to a 2011 Immigration and Customs Enforcement memo.

Peñalosa presented Sixto's situation to the church board in April 2016, and the board agreed to offer sanctuary. Then, in May, the Ninth U.S. Circuit Court of Appeals lifted a stay of removal, paving the way for Sixto's deportation.

Peñalosa called Sixto. It's time to go into sanctuary, Sixto recalls him saying.

Sixto was installing a roof. He didn't know anything about roofing when he started in the early 1990s. Now he does. He can shape any piece of metal, any kind of material. Just ask him and he'll do it. He's worked with Mexican tile, Eagle tile, clay tile. He has done roofs on army bases and schools and in residential neighborhoods. He'll build you a roof from scratch, if you want.

I feel his pride. But on that May morning last year, no one

cared about his expertise. He was an illegal alien. He stopped working and called his boss. I have to leave and go into sanctuary, he said. I have to quit my job.

That feels long ago now. How many months has he been at Shadow Rock? Sixto asks himself. Seven, eight?

"Eight," I say. Sixto looks at me and shakes his head. He smiles, the sadness in his eyes unmistakable. His daughters, Cynthia and Alondra, both college graduates, and his five-year-old son, Ian, visit him at least once a week. He tells his daughters, Leave your phones at home. Be with me, don't text your friends. I don't see you that much. Ian scampers around Sixto's room, checks out whatever captures his interest—a filing cabinet, a desk, Sixto's bed. He got a toy for Christmas that rises and whirs in the air like a helicopter. It bounces off the walls. Sixto watches Ian, feels the time they have left with each other slipping away. They talk on the phone all the time but it's not the same. Not the same at all.

Sixto doesn't call too many people. He telephones his daughters every day. They text photos of Ian. If he gets into trouble at school, the girls let Sixto know. For instance, Ian likes to play with food. Throws it. Sixto tells him food is not a toy. It is not for throwing. If you take it, eat it. And listen to your teachers, to your mother.

Sixto shows me a row of numbers separated by plus signs on the whiteboard. He teaches Ian math. The boy is very smart, Sixto says. At Christmastime, Sixto helped Ian write a letter to Santa Claus. Tell him what you need, he told his son. The boy asked for a Batman mask and cape. He added, *Please Santa Claus get my father out of the church.*

Ian asks his father, Why are there so many trees? Who makes

the rocks? Why is the sky so blue? Why is there snow? Who makes the parks? When do you leave here?

Ken Heintzelman, pastor of Shadow Rock United Church of Christ, sits in his office on a Saturday afternoon and waits for my questions. His office overlooks a road that wends its way downhill from the triangular church. A passing driver would see the light from an electric candle in one of the church windows, indicating that an individual has sought sanctuary.

I ask Ken when he first met Sixto. He peers at me through his glasses and strokes his goatee. He recalls the night Sixto and Peñalosa attended the April board meeting. Peñalosa said that an order of deportation was very possible and he expected a decision any day. Sixto might very well need sanctuary. He was a good candidate, a family man, a homeowner. Employed. Had never been in legal trouble. Ken and the board considered his request. They concluded that immigration authorities were not considering the life he had established in Phoenix. How could he be expected to walk away from it? The board agreed to let him move into the church.

Shadow Rock began offering sanctuary in 2014. That year, the church joined the New Sanctuary Movement (NSM), a growing faith-based initiative that now involves up to 120 congregations across the country, about a quarter of them ready to provide residential protection to people at risk of deportation. NSM is heir to the 1980s sanctuary movement, which dissolved after the Phoenix Immigration and Customs Enforcement office stopped granting stays of deportation without explanation. Even removal orders resulting from administrative errors and negligent attorneys were no longer being overturned.

Shadow Rock had given sanctuary to three Mexican men before the congregation agreed to take in Sixto. Although Phoenix does not count itself among the nation's more than two hundred sanctuary cities, none of the Shadow Rock cases, Ken tells me, have been challenged by immigration authorities. ICE determined that the men did not pose a national security threat. They had no criminal records, so the agency did not consider their cases a priority for deportation.

These days, however, Ken worries. On February 15, 2017, the city council voted against Phoenix opting for sanctuary city status. In addition, President Donald Trump has threatened to crack down on the sanctuary movement. If he does, Ken says, people like Sixto will be vulnerable. ICE will know where to find them. The Shadow Rock congregation will respond— how, Ken doesn't know. He shifts in his chair and stares at the ceiling, disturbed, I think, by the thought.

I ask him about Sixto's first evening in the church. Another Mexican man, Ismael Delgado, who stayed in sanctuary at Shadow Rock for more than four hundred days, let Sixto in when he first arrived. Sixto appeared very guarded. Ken and the congregation left him alone to adjust. They did not want to come across as "gringo do-gooders."

Ken gave Sixto things to do when he asked, careful not to give the impression that he was indentured labor. He also offered him the church keys. Sixto was welcome to go where he pleased on the property. The keys were a matter of practicality. He had to be able to move around the church like anyone else. If Ken couldn't trust him with the keys, why would he let him stay?

As long as Sixto has patience, Ken thinks he will persevere. The church, he says, is guided in part by the parable of the persistent widow from the Book of Luke. In the parable, the widow pleads with a judge to grant her justice against an adversary. For some time the judge refuses, but finally he says to himself, "Even though I don't fear God or care what people think, yet because this widow keeps bothering me, I will see that she gets justice, so that she won't eventually come and attack me!" And the Lord said, "Listen to what the unjust judge says. And will not God bring about justice for his chosen ones, who cry out to him day and night? Will he keep putting them off? I tell you, he will see that they get justice, and quickly."

Sixto grew up in Sonora, Mexico, one of nine children. His father farmed land that belonged to another man before he bought his own farm. Their house was so small, so tiny, Sixto recalls. When he was seven years old, he began to work in the fields. They grew wheat, cotton, oranges, lemons. Different things for different seasons. He attended school, took care of cows, sheep, and goats. He completed his homework in the fields. His parents did not know how to read or write. They had no money to send him to college. His father was short but powerful. He would tell Sixto, Be a man. Be strong. Sixto's mother took care of the daughters; his father watched Sixto and his brothers. Sit up straight at the table, he'd say. Eat and be quiet. Eat whatever your mother serves. Throw nothing away. No elbows on the table. Don't come to the table without a shirt—this is not a bar. When you talk to someone, look them in the eye, show them respect. Don't say bad words. Sixto's father would smack him if he cussed. He would warn him two times. If he didn't listen, he got the back of the hand to his mouth.

Sixto caught rides to a school about twenty-five miles away.

He'd leave home at six in the morning and get there an hour later by bus. He'd eat a cheese and egg tortilla for breakfast.

A family friend lived close to the school and gave him bread and cheese for lunch.

His father called his mother *guerrera*, warrior, because she worked hard and was fiercely protective of her children. When they got sick, she would walk them to a clinic almost fifteen miles away. She carried them when they were toddlers. Sixto wonders how she did it. Today, people don't do anything without a car.

In 1986, an older brother moved to Arizona and told Sixto to join him. His mother rode with Sixto from Sonora north on a train nicknamed *El Burro*, because it was so slow. Sixto never forgot how his mother cried at the thought of another son leaving her. He jumped the border fence near Nogales. There was no barbed wire on it in those days, Sixto says. The border patrol didn't bother with him. He caught a ride to Phoenix on the back of a motorcycle. He was sixteen and spoke no English. He had never been in a city, had never seen streets so wide, buildings so tall. He had never left his family. He felt scared and exhilarated.

He worked as a landscaper his first six years in Phoenix. He cut grass, learned how to use a Weed Eater. The work reminded him of his family's farm. The hot weather was the same as in Sonora. In Phoenix, however, he had air-conditioning. A shower replaced the bucket of water he had used to bathe. A forty-hour workweek gave him enough money to buy new shoes. In Mexico he would have had to work much longer just to buy a pair of pants. He sent $150 a month to his family.

Sixto left landscaping in 1992 to work in a warehouse, where he packaged waterbed frames and met the mother of his children. She, too, had grown up in Sonora. They lived together and had two daughters, but never married. They separated after ten years. A failed attempt at reconciliation produced Ian.

In 1998, a friend approached Sixto about a job. He said a company was hiring roofers.

I've never done that, Sixto said.

That's okay. You'll learn.

How much will he pay? Sixto asked.

How much do you want to make?

Give me ten dollars an hour.

His first three months as a roofer, blisters developed on Sixto's mouth and hands from the sun. He wore a long-sleeved shirt and cap to protect himself, but his skin still burned. He sweltered but he enjoyed the work, the sense of accomplishment in assembling a new roof. The guys called him *viejo*, old, because of his wrinkled forehead.

In the summer of 2012, his boss sent him to Baltimore. He drove. He liked what he saw of Missouri, Tennessee, and West Virginia. So green. Very different from Sonora and Arizona. For three months he worked ten hours a day, five days a week, installing roofs, and eight hours on Saturday. He visited Washington, DC, and appreciated its wide streets. Baltimore streets, he thought, were too narrow. People complained about the ninety-degree heat, but Sixto thought it was nothing. Arizona reached one hundred and more. He worked with metal in that kind of heat. Metal was bad but copper was worse, it absorbed more.

Since he's been at the church, guys he worked with in Baltimore and Phoenix call him. We have a lot of work, they tell him. We miss you. He feels good when they call. They know he's a hard worker. They were a good team.

What's going on? his friends ask. Why are you living at a church?

In 2009, Sixto drove to Yuma for a roofing job. On his return to Phoenix, traffic slowed for a border patrol checkpoint. At that time, he no longer had a work permit. He had stayed in Arizona because it had become his home. He knew that he always risked being stopped.

Do you have papers? Sixto recalls one of the patrolmen asking him.

No.

You can't stay here if you can't show you're here legally. When was the last time you were in Mexico?

2000.

How'd you enter the U.S.?

I had a work permit then.

What color was it?

Red, he answered correctly.

How long you here?

Twenty-five years.

Why don't you have papers?

They said I couldn't have them anymore.

Okay.

The border patrol held him two to three hours. He was taken to a county jail near Yuma until he was dropped off at the ICE detention center in Florence, Arizona. He had never been detained before. People from Mexico, Guatemala, El Salvador, Honduras, the Dominican Republic, and the Philippines filled the center. Sixto felt bad for the families. Fathers stayed in one section, their kids and wives in another. The kids cried. There were a lot of kids, two to three years old up to five, and babies. A bad experience for kids, Sixto thought. They don't understand.

Who's hungry? the guards would say.

Sixto and other detainees would raise a hand.

Come here. Okay, take all these.

Sixto and the other volunteers carried boxes of Maruchan Instant Lunch ramen noodle soup to the detainees in their cell block. He slept in a cold room. The light reflecting off the white walls gave him a headache. He never saw the sun. The noise of doors closing, people shouting, overwhelmed him. The plastic plates smelled. The guards served Kool-Aid. Most of the detainees got frustrated and agreed to sign out and be deported. Sixto's mother visited him and cried. She never thought one of her sons would be in a place she considered a jail.

Sixto got to know one Filipino man who appeared before an immigration judge. The judge, Sixto says, ordered him to leave the country. That night the man fell out of the top bunk of a bed and injured himself. He was transferred to a hospital, thus delaying his deportation.

Then there was this guy from Mexico. He called his wife and told her to sell their car and truck to pay the rent.

Hey, Sixto, the guy said. Give me two thousand dollars for my car. If you get out before me, give the money to my wife.

No, I don't want the car, Sixto said.

Fifteen days later the guy was released. Another man's wife made tamales to pay the rent.

Three weeks after he was detained, Sixto was released with

an order to appear before a Phoenix immigration judge. He had lost ten pounds. He returned home and hired Peñalosa. He was allowed a work permit while his case went through the courts.

"I'm here," he'd tell his family. "I'm not going anywhere."

In October 2012, Cynthia Paz, then eighteen, testified before an immigration judge that if her father was deported she would suffer financial and emotional hardship. She said he provided child support for Ian and also helped care for him. Alondra, fifteen, testified that she had a good relationship with her father and that he supported her financially and emotionally. Sixto testified that he had lived in the United States since 1986. He owned a home and paid a mortgage of $812 a month. He owned a 2003 Chevy and a 2008 Dodge heavy-duty truck. He had a 401(k) plan worth about $8,000. He had about $600 in savings. He paid child support. He had studied English for eight months at a community college. When asked by the court if he could find work in Mexico, Sixto testified that the roofing systems he installed and the building materials he used would not be available there. He did not think he could support his family. Sixto argued that the court should not underestimate the importance of a father to the lives of his children.

The court found that Sixto and his daughters provided credible testimony. It did not, however, conclude that his children would suffer "unconscionable" hardship should he be deported. The court denied Sixto's application.

In March 2014, the Board of Immigration Appeals affirmed the court's decision and gave Sixto sixty days to voluntarily leave the United States. Sixto sought a stay of removal from the

Department of Homeland Security. The department denied his request but determined that he was not a priority for removal, citing his lack of a criminal record. He remained in Arizona.

In February 2015, Cynthia turned twenty-one and submitted a family petition on behalf of her father. U.S. Citizenship and Immigration Services, the benefits arm of the Department of Homeland Security, approved the petition and granted Sixto a work permit. But ICE, the department's enforcement unit, opposed the motion to reopen and convinced the Board of Immigration Appeals not to consider the case. Sixto then turned to the Ninth U.S. Circuit Court of Appeals. When the court denied his request in May 2016, he walked into Shadow Rock Church.

"With a case like this, we need the community to support us and pressure the authorities," Peñalosa told me. "Just me and the church advocating for Sixto is not going to persuade them. It's unfortunate, but that's how it is."

Sixto's daughter Cynthia remembers that her father took her and Alondra to a mall the night he told them he might have to move into Shadow Rock. He broke the news as he looked for a parking spot. It was his only option, he said. Cynthia cried. She'd had a high school friend who had been deported as soon as she started driving. Her friend had been heading home from work and got stopped. That was it. She was gone.

Cynthia feels very close to her father. She doesn't understand why the immigration court and the Department of Homeland Security would not accept her petition. She worries about him. He's not the type of person to sit around and do nothing. Sanctuary sounded like a prison. She works as a medical assistant. When would she have time to see him? Only weekends?

When Sixto told his boss he had to go into sanctuary, his boss told him to seek the advice of a lawyer. Sixto told him he had a lawyer and that his lawyer had just called and said to get to Shadow Rock. Sixto finished the day's roofing job and drove home. He showered, grabbed a change of clothes, and his brother drove him to the church. When he left his house, Sixto felt weird, sad. He couldn't believe it. As he looked out the window of the truck, he already felt separated from the world. He had never expected this, not after having lived in Phoenix for so long. Everything seemed to be on his side, and then it wasn't. Good job, his family doing well—what happened? He didn't understand.

Ismael met him at the church and let him in. Your case is easy, everything will work out, he told Sixto. Ismael showed him his room. Sixto lay down and stared at the ceiling in the dark. He told himself, *This is not my home.*

The next morning, he woke up at six. He walked around the church, wandered up the cactused hills behind it, and watched the sun rise and shadows retreat like water pulled back from shore by an undertow. In the light he noticed that someone had vandalized a table near the church playground. Maybe he could fix it. Something to do.

Sixto's life soon fell into a pattern. Ismael helped him establish a routine. Get up early, drink coffee. Shower, slip on a T-shirt, jeans. Run a comb through his head of thick dark hair. Shave and trim his mustache. Read the Bible, make breakfast. Walk around outside. BS with Ismael, watch a little TV, play basketball on the court in back of the church. Help with general maintenance. Sometimes people from the congregation dropped by and wished him well. Everything happens for a reason, he told himself.

He and Ismael talked about what they would do when they won their court cases and left the church. They'd organize a big fiesta. They'd butcher a calf and cook all day. They'd get ice and buy a lot of beer and invite all their friends. Travel the country and visit all the people in sanctuary. They agreed that the first to leave Shadow Rock would help the one left behind.

Days passed, then weeks and months. Sixto had told his brother he'd be in sanctuary for two weeks max, but the authorities refused to reopen Sixto's case. Soon it was November, then December. Christmas was weeks away and Sixto missed his family more than ever. So did Ismael, but he caught a break. His lawyer had reached an arrangement with ICE. Ismael could go home.

Like Sixto, Ismael is stocky and has short black hair combed to one side. He laughs easily. He has lived in the States since 1991. He owns his home, is married, and has a daughter.

Ismael's problems with immigration began when the police stopped him in 2009 for a traffic violation. They checked his ID and saw that he was undocumented. He then had three court hearings in six years. In 2015, an immigration judge gave him sixty days to voluntarily leave the country. A lawyer advised him to seek sanctuary at Shadow Rock. After six months of living in the church, Ismael met with his attorney to discuss his options. As they talked, Ismael mentioned that he and his brother had been mugged at gunpoint in 2008. His lawyer told him he was eligible for a U visa, a nonimmigrant visa for victims of crimes. Ismael applied.

In December 2016, during a Sunday church service, Ismael's lawyer announced to the Shadow Rock congregation that ICE had determined that Ismael could remain in Phoenix without threat of deportation while authorities reviewed his U visa application. Ismael had not expected the announcement. He embraced Sixto. He knew what his friend was feeling. Sixto would be alone now. Ismael promised to visit.

The morning he left, Sixto patted Ismael on the back like a father encouraging a son.

Don't be afraid, he said. They prayed together. Sixto watched Ismael's wife drive him away.

Alondra Paz is nineteen but looks much younger. She remembers a high school friend whose mother was deported to Mexico. Her friend would tell Alondra about her mother and cry. Maybe she'll come back, Alondra would say, but she didn't believe it.

Her father, Alondra recalls, liked to play pranks when she was younger. They'd walk into a store and if he didn't see someone standing at the counter, he would ring the bell long and hard. When the salesperson appeared, he'd say Alondra had rung it. The kid in him came out all the time. He was very supportive too. He attended all of Alondra's soccer and softball games.

Alondra never saw her father as a citizen or a noncitizen. He was her dad, no more, no less. He wasn't different from other dads. Everything he had he earned. It never occurred to her that he might be deported.

He used to go out of town for a lot of roofing jobs. One time, he said he was going to Maryland. If anything happens to me, stay calm, be strong, he said. Alondra was very young then, but she had a sense that he wasn't talking about getting hurt on the job or injured in a car accident. It was something else, something bigger. She didn't understand. She thinks now her father knew that one day he would face an immigration judge. After the border patrol stopped him in Yuma, Sixto called Alondra and Cynthia from Florence. Everything will be fine, he said.

Alondra attended her father's court hearings. She was so mad. Did the judge not have a family? She could barely contain herself. She thought it was cruel. In 2016 she graduated from college, a month after her father had entered sanctuary. He couldn't attend her graduation. So sad, she says, that he was not there to hug her. She came to the church afterward.

I graduated, she told him. It wasn't the same. She would never have a photo of him with her in her cap and gown. I know, he told her. She showed him her diploma. She had worked hard, had gotten good grades.

Sometimes Alondra receives calls from strangers. They ask, Where is your father? Text messages too, with the same question. Alondra has no idea who these people are, what they want.

Christmas 2016. Ismael was gone. Sixto had never felt so lonely. He missed everything about his family. Going to church. Watching them open their presents. The big dinner. The laughter, the hugs. He paced back and forth like a chained dog. It was his first Christmas without them. He tried to read the Bible but he could not concentrate. *Why, why?* he asked himself. He didn't have any answer. The only answer was to stay at Shadow Rock. His daughters visited and brought Ian. That helped. New Year's Day was better. His brother stayed with him for three days and they ate tamales and posole. When his brother left, Sixto felt like garbage. Alone again. He had busted his ass all these years and hadn't done anything wrong, and yet someone high above him said he had. He wasn't a criminal but he was being treated like one. Sometimes he thought he should just go. Leave the church, feel better. But go where? Once a week a church volunteer works with him on his English. He speaks English, but he wants to improve. Some verbs in the past and present tenses throw him.

A gray owl crashed into a church window the other night. Sixto heard a hard noise. He walked around the church with a flashlight and found the dazed owl in a window well. He photographed it with his cell phone and then carried it to the branch of a small tree to save it from coyotes. He decided that branch wasn't high enough and moved it to another. The owl gripped the branch with its talons. It turned its head to Sixto, its big eyes unblinking. In the morning it was gone.

Arlene Dominguez, the director of Shadow Rock Sanctuary Ministry and a member of the church for the past twenty-five years, meets with Sixto almost every day. She tells me that every sanctuary case is different. The second man the church provided sanctuary to was single and had no family in the States, yet ICE decided not to remove him. Sixto has a family, a job, pays taxes, and has lived in Phoenix for a long time, but ICE wants to throw him out. Arlene doesn't get it.

This morning she ate breakfast with him. Burger King, Sixto's favorite. He had hoped to repair the church roof. Ismael was going to come by and help but then it started raining. Too bad. Arlene likes seeing Ismael. When he visits, he wanders the halls like a dog sniffing old scents. He can't believe he spent more than a year here. Better stay inside, Arlene told Sixto. You don't want to get on a ladder and slip and fall.

I ask Arlene if she moved to Phoenix from Mexico. No,

she tells me, she was born in Arizona, has lived here all her life. Her mother also. Her father hails from Texas. Arlene's paternal grandfather had an extended family in Juárez, and Arlene and her parents and siblings would visit them. Arlene can remember the tiny house where eight of her cousins and aunts and uncles lived. They all worked in hotels, cleaning. When the kids were old enough, they worked in hotels too. Arlene's life might have been no different had she not been born in the States.

The other day Arlene spent a weekend in Rocky Point, Mexico, a place sometimes called Arizona's beach getaway. All these luxurious hotels. Beyond the hotels, she saw Mexican men and women living in shacks. A friend told her they earn about seventy dollars a week as laborers.

"You can't live on that," Arlene says. "They come here for a chance." She doesn't think they're asking a whole lot.

Periodically, Shadow Rock offers shelter to homeless people, and Sixto helps set up cots. They can stay about one week. Sixto talks to them. They ask him if they can use the restroom or take a bottle of water. Yes, why not? Sixto tells them. Take what you need. He remembers one family with two daughters and two grandsons. They avoided talking to him. They didn't speak Spanish and he thinks they assumed he wouldn't understand them. He felt their discomfort and left them alone.

In an arrangement ICE made with the church, immigrant families released from the Florence detention center can stay at Shadow Rock for a few days if they have no other place to go. They come from all over, Sixto says. Honduras, El Salvador, Guatemala, Nicaragua. Some speak only Mayan dialect, and

Sixto doesn't understand them. Others ask to call family in the States. Sixto lets them use his phone. While he waited to appear in immigration court, one guy was going to stay with relatives in Idaho, another in Iowa, still another in Texas. Sixto listens to their stories. It took some of them two weeks to cross Mexico to the U.S. border. One man said he paid a coyote eight thousand dollars. The coyote took the money and called the man's family and demanded more.

What are you doing here? a Honduran man asked Sixto.

They want to send me to Mexico.

Why? What did you do?

Nothing. I've lived here twenty-five years.

You have too many years here. Why would they send you away?

Because they want to.

Sixto spends part of each day meditating. He sits outside on a rock overlooking the basketball court for hours. He notices people walking on a nearby street. He sees people driving, leading regular lives, while he can't go anywhere.

He thinks about his eighty-six-year-old father and his mother. Sixto worries that his father might die before he can leave the church. His parents were sick his first month in sanctuary. His mother has diabetes; his father wasn't eating. Sixto wants his father to know Ian. He thinks of his son. Ian needs him. A week before my arrival, Ian had stayed with Sixto for a few days. Ian played—indoor golf, baseball, football, basketball. He raced around on a scooter. He watched his father dig a drainage ditch and picked small rocks out of the trench. When Sixto finished digging, he began work on the playground. He replaced sand that had washed away with a recent rain and fixed the steps to a slide. Then Ian went home.

Sixto thinks about his job. There's a lot of roofing work in Phoenix. His boss is looking for people. He doesn't have enough workers.

Letting out a long breath, Sixto stares at the sky. He sees falcons circling, no clouds. Tranquillity. He closes his eyes. He glides on invisible currents. He feels air. He feels freedom.

Fishing with the King

F.J. Campo sits at a table with two receipt books. He sells fuel and bait to fishermen from his Shell Beach, Louisiana, marina, scrawling the day's date, April 20, 2010, on each receipt he writes. A fan circulates the odor of the freshly cut plywood boards he used to expand his bait shop. He plans to put two large bait tanks near the new bathroom.

A shrimp boat floats by on the other side of the dock past tall marsh grasses where a raccoon squats rubbing its front paws together in the water, and F.J. waves at the crew. Bars of yellow light layer the water and heat shimmers on the shoreline. The sky blindingly blue.

F.J. recalls trawling for shrimp when he was twelve. He had told his father to take care of the family store: F.J. would do the fishing from then on. In those days, everything was done by hand. No mechanical winches like now. He had always wanted to be on the water. Fresh air. No putting up with smart alecks. No road rage. A freedom most people don't have. Have to be self-motivated though. You got to drag your ass out of bed at 4 a.m. Some people can't get up at 8 a.m., and if they do they need an alarm clock to do it.

It's a life of long hours. Work five in the morning to six at night. Home if he's lucky by seven. Not much time off. F.J. works year-round, gets maybe two weeks off in January to hunt deer. His daddy did the same thing, as did his granddaddy. It's a way of life. You either grow up with shrimp between your toes or they grow there on their own. The only thing F.J. wanted out of was school. When he graduated from high school in 1960, he never looked back.

Two quarts' oil, F.J., a fishermen shouts.

Okay.

F.J. jots down the amount in his book. Honor system. Guys'll drop in with a check once in a while. Casual. One guy this morning came in after doing six months in jail for breaking someone's jaw in a bar fight. Guess you hit him too hard, huh? F.J. says. Better to shoot someone. You'd get out of that. The fisherman owes him $708. Not bad.

On the radio, F.J. overhears something about an oil rig that blew up. Deepwater something. Belongs to BP. Okay, so? Not the first spill, won't be the last. Hurricanes and spills. There's always something.

Fifty gallons' gas, F.J.

Okay.

That evening F.J. drives home on the twisting snake strip of pavement that is the only road in Shell Beach. He smells the damp wood of docked oyster and shrimp boats. He smells the salt-wet air and the odor of fish and fuel and wet nets mixed together. He sees sky-surfing seagulls, hears their calls, and never tires of any of it although he has been awake since before dawn and was greeted by the same sights and smells then as he is now and will be again tomorrow and the day after and for all the days that follow. He wouldn't have it any other way.

At home, he sinks into a living room chair and flips on the TV. See what the fuck happened today. Eleven people killed, burned up in that oil rig explosion. That bothers him. Their kids, wives, fathers, mothers will never see them again. Bodies incinerated to ash. How do they say goodbye? If he was given a choice of burning to death or killing his best friend, F.J. has no doubt he'd say, Sorry buddy, and blow his friend's brains out.

This can't be good, F.J. thinks.

FISH WITH THE KING
(sign near the Campo marina)

He was the firstborn and named Frank Campo Jr. after his father. F.J. for short. A big boy, big as a spider monkey. His mother had cried from the pain of birthing for four days after he was born.

His father's people came to New Orleans from Barcelona, Spain, by way of the Canary Islands. Frank Campo Sr. was nicknamed Blackie because of his dark Castilian skin and volatile Latin temper.

F.J.'s mother's family was also from Barcelona. They took a ship directly to New Orleans, where his grandmother was born nine days after their arrival.

The Campos settled in Shell Beach, a fishing community about forty miles from New Orleans. In the 1780s, Spanish Canary Islanders, or Isleños, settled in the area after receiving land grants from Spain. After selling their land to the planters, the Isleños frequently worked on the plantations they had helped create. Some began to resettle in the easternmost reaches of St. Bernard Parish around the 1820s, which led to the establishment of the Delacroix Island fishing community before the Civil War. F.J.'s mother was raised on Delacroix Island, about thirty miles east of Shell Beach.

By the 1900s Shell Beach was a thriving community. Seafood harvested by its fishermen in the 1800s and 1900s supplied New Orleans restaurants with a seemingly inexhaustible amount of shrimp, fish, and crabs. F.J.'s grandfather, Celestino, started a business catering to sportfishermen in the early 1900s, guiding, renting skiffs, and providing live bait. Blackie went to work for his father when he was ten and never left the business, despite hardships arising from hurricanes and development. The dredging of the Mississippi River–Gulf Outlet in the early 1960s forced the village to move inland about one mile from the Lake Borgne shoreline. The Campo home and business were destroyed by hurricanes on four occasions. Yet the Campos rebuilt each time, even after Hurricane Katrina tore everything out of Shell Beach except building slabs.

"I know there's nothing left, but when I finally got back here I felt good for the first time since the storm hit, because I felt like I was finally home," Blackie Campo told the *Times-Picayune* newspaper in June 2006 when he and his wife, Mabel, moved into a FEMA trailer in Shell Beach after spending ten months with family in Baton Rouge. "I can see the water and smell the marsh. This is where I belong."

F.J. was born in 1942. When he was barely more than a toddler, he watched his grandfather sell gas for six cents a gallon. He had a big old red tank, a hand pump with a glass tube, the gallons marked on it. Couldn't sell but five gallons at a time. His father took out fishing parties that included celebrities like trumpet player and bandleader Al Hirt, and Blackie would sometimes meet Hirt in Las Vegas to watch Muhammad Ali fight. He threw dice in the casinos to pay for his trip.

In those days, F.J.'s grandfather towed two skiffs behind

a big boat. When the fishing party reached deep water, they would row the skiffs to where they wanted to fish. Hours later, they rowed back to the big boat with their catch. The big boat had a Johnson outboard motor and went only seven, eight miles an hour. It had an updraft carburetor that gave the old man all kinds of fits. Nothing then was very reliable, except his grandmother's home brew. Goddamn house was full of it. She kept all the shutters and doors wide open, and consequently the sheriff never suspected anything improper going on. Ain't got to check this one, he'd say. It never occurred to him that she might be hiding something. Instead, he stopped at houses with curtained windows and locked doors, indicators in his mind of potential impropriety. Busted everybody around F.J.'s grandmother's place until nobody had any home brew but her. Back rooms full of that shit. She cleaned up. Slick old bird, his grandmother.

F.J.'s godfather owned a boat with a flathead motor. One day the motor wouldn't start and he got all pissed off. F.J., still a boy, watched him take a hatchet and break off the distributor. Swung again and took out the carburetor. Again. Took out the plugs. Walked to a hardware store and bought new plugs, distributor, and carburetor. F.J. tagged along. Back on the boat, his godfather rebuilt the engine and got that bad boy going. If I'd I had an ax in here instead of a hatchet, I'd've finished it in one swing, he told F.J.

That kind of shit makes an impression, F.J. says.

On July 5, 2010, the U.S. Fish and Wildlife Service shut down Lake Borgne about seven, eight miles away from F.J.'s marina and where most of the Shell Beach fishermen trawled for shrimp. F.J. blames the weather. Storms the week of July 4 did them in. Northeast winds make high water. It's like putting a match to gas. The storm blew for four days and rolled all that oil in and closed fishing areas down. That's what did them in. That first summer storm, and it wasn't anything compared to what they normally get.

The feds told F.J. to stop selling bait. Now he only distributes fuel to fishermen hired by BP to lay boom and stop the oil from reaching the marshes. A company working for BP wants to rent his marina, put in computers and all that stuff.

I'll tell you how it's going to be, the company rep began, before F.J. interrupted him.

No, F.J. said. *I'll* tell *you* how it's going to be. This is my dock. I'm the king here.

The man left, never to come by again.

The fishermen arrive at five every morning for a briefing with BP contractors in a trailer across from F.J.'s marina. Shadowy figures sip cups of coffee, hesitant in the half-light between morning and the receding night. A sign on the road reads: *Restricted Area.* Only fishermen participating in the cleanup can enter. At the briefing, the fishermen are told where in the Gulf to put boom that day, where to patrol for tar balls, where to look for oil. Each fisherman has an ID card with their photograph, name, and a bar code.

Before all this shit, the fishermen complain, they used to wake up, get out on the water and where they had to be by seven, and work until noon. Have lunch, drink a beer, get back to work. Catch you thirty, forty sacks of shrimp and go home happy. Got the day's catch. Not now. They're working for BP. If you're not needed, you got to show up anyway and sit around from five to six on standby. Fishermen aren't used to being told what to do and then not have anything to do.

After the briefing, a woman employed by BP enters F.J.'s marina and sits across from him with a palm-size scanner. When a fisherman docks his boat for gas, she scans his bar code and then types in the amount of fuel and oil he bought. She writes the information down in a notebook and F.J. writes it down in a receipt book. She downloads her data at the end of each day. F.J. doesn't know why she has to keep track of the same thing he keeps track of. She leaves at 5 p.m. but he remains open until 6, so their paperwork never matches. The woman agrees that her work is pointless.

I'm getting paid for a useless job, she says.

Everything's screwed up. Fishermen have told F.J. that the dock in Hopedale, only five minutes away, sells gasoline mixed with water. They figure the supplier must be trying to stretch it to get every dime he can. Looks like Gatorade and tears up an engine. They refer to Hopedale as hell. Where you going today? I'm going to hell. The smart ones drive their boats four miles just to buy gas from F.J.

Hey, F.J.

Yeah?

It says here you sell oil, gas, diesel.

Yeah.

And bait. I'm going to sue you for false advertising.

Call BP.

Guys who have fished for years can't get their boats on the cleanup list. They could be paid nearly one thousand dollars a day or more, depending on the size of their boat and whether it's used to distribute boom or skim oil. Other guys who've never fished in their lives get their boats on the list like it was nothing. They have money, F.J. figures. You got a crew boat? Yeah. Give me fifty dollars a day and I'll get you listed. It's always been that way in Louisiana. Kickbacks. F.J. sees more people walking around with *duh* on their faces than he can count.

Hey, F.J., you got any bait?

They won't let me sell it.

I don't know where else to go.

Home or a casino 'bout the only shot you got.

The other day, F.J. got so strung out he was liable to shoot someone. BP had him order all this gas and diesel, but no one gave him any money to pay for it. It was his name on the $29,000 tab. His debt. He went to the parish president. I'm buying a lock, he said. If I have no money tomorrow, I'm going to put a lock on my door and I'm not selling anybody any fuel.

You can't do that.

Don't tell me what I can't do, F.J. told him. I'm the king here. I set the rules.

The next morning, a check was delivered. Damn, how about that? F.J. said.

F.J. considers himself fortunate to have been shut down two and a half months after the spill. He knows people up and down the coast who haven't shrimped or fished for a month and more. He can't reach them. They don't answer their phones. He hears about guys going home and arguing with the old lady. Couples didn't fight before. Not like this.

Better save money, F.J., his accountant told him. If BP leaves today and there's no more fish, what are you going to do? Might be two years from now when BP goes, but it could happen.

Hell, I don't know, F.J. said. I can't plan for tomorrow, let alone two years from now.

He wakes up thinking about the spill. Like his brain doesn't go to sleep anymore. He doesn't know what's going on. He used to figure out shit when he was asleep. Now he doesn't. No one sits around and bullshits anymore. No one gets together. Nobody's home anymore. Everyone is working different rotations. This isn't who they are.

Hey, F.J.

Yeah.

Remember that commercial in the seventies with the Indian shedding a tear because his river's dirty? You could do the same commercial with fishermen crying and looking at their water. What do you think?

RULES FOR SHRIMPING
Stay out until you run out of ice.
Stay out until you run out of fuel.
Stay out until you catch a load of shrimp or you get so horny you got to come home.

THINGS TO KNOW
No average income, no average trip.
Might make a load of shrimp in one day.
Might come home with nothing.

DON'T EVER FORGET
It pays well. Twelve-, thirteen-year-olds making $600 a week working with their daddies.

Put an old-timey fisherman's soul in a young man's
body and he'd be a fucking mule, yes sir.

Outside the front door, a .270 caliber bolt-action rifle.
Above it a sign:

ASSHOLE
It's not just a word
But a way of life

Inside Alton Blappert's house, Spanish moss hanging from
the wood-beamed ceiling. Carries the scent of marsh grass and
soft motionless air.

Alton says:

Everyone knew Blackie Campo. Mr. Blackie, we called him.
I always bought my bait from him and then F.J. until this happened. Everyone knew the minute the Deepwater well blew it
was trouble. It's over with. This is our breeding season. Oil'll
kill everything off. No doubt about it. Restaurants'll shut down
too. Before the oil spill, I could walk three blocks and catch all
the fish I wanted. Not now. Everything shut down. When that
oil hits the marsh, it'll be here ten years easy. No way to clean it
when it's in the grass, no sir.

Alton sits on a broken-down couch, no springs beneath
the worn cushions to support his slight weight. He is a lean
man. Leathery muscles stretched taut as rubber bands cause
little ripples to spread beneath the skin when he moves, all
knobby elbows and knees and whiskey breath and cigarettes.
Beside him, a black cat tore up he says by a coyote the night
before. The cat sleeps. Coyotes come out of the marsh early in

the morning or late at night. Alton shoots their asses when he can, nails their furs on a post outside his house. Stiff as cardboard when raised by a breeze. Vengeance for three other cats they killed.

Don't get on the couch, he tells his four Labradors. Used to be hunting dogs. Deer, turkey, rabbit. Like Alton now retired.

The dogs get on the couch.

Alton says:

When I was a kid coming up, I liked everything about fishing, yes sir. Mainly the money. I shrimped twenty-eight years.

He stands and crosses the wood floor to the refrigerator. Removes a thick chunk of thawed chicken breast from a cutting board and skewers it on a hook the size of his palm. Hang it later from a tree for the coyotes. Swallow this hook and that's it he's done.

Alton says:

I refused to fish oysters. Hard-ass work, yes sir. One hundred pounds a sack. Not for me lifting that kind of weight. My son-in-law built a shelf to use as an oyster bed. We were expecting a good crop of oysters this year. Were, yes sir.

He shakes his head.

It'll be fifteen, twenty years before everything gets right. Soon's the oil is picked up we won't see BP no more but we'll have all this contamination, yes sir. BP pays my son-in-law $5,000 a month but he used to make $10,000 in six days' fishing.

The dogs stir on the couch. Alton fills a plastic syringe with water, squirts it down the cat's throat.

All right, you don't want any, he says when the cat breaks away from him, its back legs limp as snakes.

Alton says:

My daddy started taking me fishing when I was five years old. Shrimp, crab, mollusks, red fish, trout. Fifty-five years later I fell through an attic down to the first floor. Broke bones in my neck. That did me. Just as well. If I was still fishing I would be done for.

F.J.'s first two boats were named *Lacy Marie* and *Brandy Michelle* by their previous owner. It was bad luck to change the names. It was bad luck to bring bananas on board too. He didn't know if he believed all that but saw no point in finding out. He called his first boat *Lady Gloria* after his wife. When they divorced, he renamed it *Miss Cathy Ann* for his daughter. A wife may not always be your wife, but a daughter will always be your daughter, he says.

On a Wednesday evening, fisherman George Barasich drives his pickup through the streets of Arabi, a New Orleans suburb about a forty-minute drive from Shell Beach. Green balled-up shrimp nets bounce in the back.

Sure, he knows F.J., knew his old man better, though. Mr. Blackie'd give you the shirt off his back. Literally. One time, maybe in January, a fisherman showed up for fuel in a T-shirt. What was he thinking? Goose bumps the size of chicken eggs. Mr. Blackie didn't say anything, just took off his wool shirt and gave it to him. Next morning he found it on his dock hanging from a hook with a note in the breast pocket: *Thanks.*

George commutes between Arabi and Baton Rouge, where his wife and daughter live. He's not going to lie. Things are not going all that well between them. It is what it is. Hurricane

Katrina tore families apart. Ain't like this oil spill's going to bring them together again.

At an intersection, a homeless man holds a sign that reads: *Help a vet. I'll work for food.* He notices the shrimp nets and asks George if he could spare a few shrimp for a meal.

They shut me down, George says.

That's sad, the homeless man says. Where're shrimp going to come from?

Texas.

Galveston?

Sure. The oil's moving that way but it's offshore.

Good luck.

You too.

George drives through the intersection, passes house after empty house still scarred from the ravages of Hurricane Katrina. Spray-painted circles and slashes show that firefighters searched these houses for survivors. Numbers beside the slashes indicate how many bodies were found. Five years later, the numbers have faded and broken windows let in the summer drizzle that gathers in pools and spills through cracks in the walls, filling the vacant houses with the sound of their ruin.

Oil might kill shrimp but it won't become part of their tissue, so there's no reason to shut me down, George says. You eat one, you won't get sick. Oysters are different. Shouldn't eat them, they'll retain the oil.

Oh hell. Who will listen? Crazy for BP not to have had a contingency plan. They all ought to be shot. At fifty-four, George never in all his days shrimping expected to see such a thing.

He last shrimped in Lake Borgne on July 2. In three hours, he hauled in three hundred pounds of shrimp. Then he turned on his radio and listened to the news. The announcer said Lake Borgne had been shut down. Oh shit, we're illegal, George said. He cleaned his nets, docked his boat, and cooked up a big seafood platter. Sat in his boat and ate with his two-man crew until it started raining. Might be the last time I go fishing, he said to the crew as much as to himself.

It's like somebody died. Same feeling but worse. Knowing he's not debt-free adds to his worries. His solvency depended on making enough money each month fishing. That's out the door. He feels anxious and sick at the loss of doing what he loves. The thrill of the chase. The ability to be on the water. Fighting Mother Nature. He really doesn't want to work for BP but he can't sit around three or four years. Can't let his family suffer. Take an ass-kicking first before that happens.

You got shrimp? a man shouts from outside one of the Katrina-destroyed homes.

They shut me down, brother, George says.

After the fishermen came in for the night, after they drove home and showered, they would stop by the house of Miss Jonsie. She made bread this big around, F.J. says. She served coffee and melted butter and the men gathered on her porch and recounted their day on the water and shot the bull. If someone said they were building a boat, the next day everyone would show up at their house with hammers and saws. Miss Jonsie didn't charge a thing. If he was a good kid, F.J. would get a hunk of bread and eat with the rest of the fishermen. Other boys who interrupted the adults got whacked on the head by whoever was closest to them. F.J. stayed quiet, listened to their stories, learned.

Lessons

You see your daddy zigzag the boat in the water?

Yeah.

You ask, Why'd you do that? He says, Bad stump, boy. Got to go around it. So when you run your own boat, you know about that stump. Or you hit it and go, Goddamn, forgot about that stump Daddy told me about. That happens.

What else?

Trout follow shrimp.

What else?

Can't drag here. Turn there. Stay on the other side of the marsh in this part. We're not turtles. This doesn't come by instinct.

We have to be taught.

Yes. You got to watch your oyster beds. Crooks know you got them. Costs a lot of money to patrol your grounds. You see the crooks go out, you go out too. Three to four times a week sometimes. You can burn thousands of dollars of gas without trying. It's expensive to watch your stuff.

What else?

You got your tides. The currents before a full moon always pick up. Good for brown shrimp. But jumbo white shrimp are the crème de la crème. When the tide is running good, use wing nets. Trawling is better in a slack tide because shrimp settle on the bottom. A slack tide and a light wind out of the southeast or east is best for sportfishermen.

What else?

Fish bite better in the morning, up until eight, nine o'clock.

Why's that?

Just is.

What else?

You can't buy what I know. You can learn it, but you can't buy it. Some people think everything's got a price. Maybe in the world they live in, but not in mine. The world I live in, that is not the case.

They sent me out with an anchor but no rope to tie it to.

They sent me out to collect tar balls without any nets. What do they want me to do? Cut a plastic milk jug in half and scoop up the balls?

These tar balls are flat. Like shit in a diaper.

They gave me swimming pool nets to scoop it out, but the current breaks the nets.

They gave me eight-foot two-by-fours to tie the boom to, but the two-by-fours are too short to hold in the marshes and they get carried away by the current. You got all this oily boom and two-by-fours floating around out there.

I came back because some asshole sent me to the wrong spot. We don't need you here. Oh goddamn. I went out here for nothing.

I know where they're sending me tomorrow. Somewhere.

It's a fucking joke.

A bad joke at that.

Forty gallons' gas, two gallons' two-stroke oil.

F.J. writes it down. His grandson Robert Campo hefts two bottles of oil from a box and tosses them to a fisherman. The gal sitting across from F.J. scans the fisherman's bar code.

Did you get that, Pa-pa?

The oil, yeah. Got it.

Robert stands on the dock near two empty bait containers, the wind whipping his hair. The dock creaks beneath his feet and he watches shrimp boats loaded with soft white booms maneuvering behind one another. Exhaust fumes dissipate in the clear air.

Robert was four when F.J. first took him on a shrimp boat. He ran around the deck playing with a toy fishing pole. By the time he was nine, he was driving the boat, handing out life jackets to sportfishermen, filling the gas tank. When he wasn't working and wasn't in school, he fished. Redfish, trout, all varieties.

Robert knows what's going on, F.J. says. *He'll remember.*

It was fun just to get out on the water and have a talk with his pa-pa. They talked about anything, really. Fishing. Family. Think we'll get any here, Pa-pa? Yeah, F.J. would say. His pa-pa thought like a fish. He knew where they would be. He knew the winds and the strength of the sun and how at different times of the morning it would send light sliding across the water while beneath its heat the fish swam and sought food.

How's everybody doing? his pa-pa would ask him. How're your cousins?

I got some real small grandkids. They won't remember like Robert.

It was on a weekend, a Friday or a Saturday, when Robert's father called him on his cell phone and told him about the spill. Robert had just come home from football practice. His father was almost crying. This ain't good, he told Robert. He didn't know what would happen. Now his father works for BP.

Robert has fished just four times since the spill, and now he can't fish at all. At least his family can still sell fuel. The Campos have been working these waters for 107 years. Robert can't fathom that much time passing. He can't fathom his family not selling bait and trawling for shrimp. No bait, people can't fish. If people don't fish, what else is there? At least his father can weld. He's a good welder.

Robert plans to attend college, play football, and major in sports medicine. He doesn't want to be like some of the fishermen he knows who drive by their old high school and stare at it like it's some sacred totem from their past. Some of them didn't even finish high school. Robert wants to be somebody.

They'll say, I was a little kid when the Deepwater well blew and I don't remember when people fished, and Robert will have to explain it to them.

Robert can still see himself with that little reedy toy fishing pole. Scampering around like the boat was one big tree fort. One of those very clear memories that feels beyond reach. When I grow up, I'm going to own my own boat and be like you, he told his father.

He doesn't think so now, no sir.

FRANK CAMPO'S MARINA
Since 1945
"The Place Where Memories Are Made"
Shell Beach * Overnight Accommodations
Gas & Diesel * Live Bait * Ice & Drinks

Hard for F.J. to believe his father has been dead for two years. Ninety. Can't live forever.

He remembers moments with his father that he hadn't thought about since he doesn't know how long. He guesses that's what death does. Leaves memories. Memories keep a man alive. He and his father used to hunt ducks in a bayou not far from Shell Beach. Don't come back here in summer, his father warned him. This bayou gets full of cottonmouth snakes. You could wear a blindfold and still kill a bunch of snakes with one shot of your gun, he said.

I don't know about all that, F.J. said.

He was about twelve years old. That summer he went back to the bayou and maneuvered into the marsh. Fucking snakes so thick they were like island grass. He turned around and ran over a bunch of them. All tangled in his motor. He had to shake them loose. Cottonmouths he knew were badass. He ran over he doesn't know how many. Afraid they'd jump in the goddamn boat.

He never told his father. Guess he knows now, F.J. says.

Two, three years ago F.J. started losing his voice. He could no longer call geese when he hunted. Last January, he lost his voice entirely. His doctor told him he had cancer of the vocal cords. Just like that, F.J. said. Just like that, his doctor said. He had an operation a short time later that has reduced his voice to a raspy whisper but removed the cancer. Whispering is better than dying.

F.J. looks like his father. The same wide chest, thick shoulders. The expressions on his face alternate between a scowl and a squint, concealing a buoyant sense of humor. He gets a kick out of sayings. *It ain't bragging if it's true.* Who said that? Jimmy Dean? F.J. doesn't know but repeats it to death, laughing each time he does, while at the same time scrutinizing those around him nose to nose to make sure they appreciate the humor too.

Big as he is, F.J. is not as big as his father. Hard to imagine that a man with hands so large he could hold a rack of fifteen billiard balls in the palm of either hand, with the cue ball set on top for good measure, would ever die. Blackie Campo bet people who refused to believe he could do such a thing. He brought home more free groceries that way than he ever spent money on. Cases of beans, sacks of rice.

God help BP if he was alive now.

Fish here and you're violated if you keep them.

Suppose' to let them go?

Yeah, they've shut all this down. Fish-and-release, it's called.

Makes no sense. Still the same water.

Fish Lake Robin?

Yeah, good fishing back there and down here.

Gotta let them go if you fish here.

Fish Hopedale Lagoon?

You can try. What they will tell you is leave, shit.

This oil's killing us.

Pay for your license and can't fish.

Get your money back.

If it was that easy, I'd stuff my firstborn back up my wife and ask for my money back.

Damn.

We'll run down to Lake Robin.

This is really messing us up.

Faded advertisements promoting different types of hunting rifles decorate the walls around the refrigerator of Alton Blappert's house. Paintings of Labradors holding dead pheasant in their mouths, a camouflaged hunter behind them. In one corner, framed black-and-white photographs show how Shell Beach once looked. Gravel streets. 1929 Ford cars. Creased faces barely revealed, fogged over. They stand on the wood-plank sidewalks caught in the viewfinder but too far away to be distinct. Ghostly blurs outside some now-vanished store.

STRESSED Spelled Backwards Is DESSERTS
(bumper sticker on the wall of the Campo marina)

Like her husband, Frank Campo Sr., Mabel Campo grew up in a family of fishermen on nearby Delacroix Island. Just about everybody was a fisherman and a trapper. She doesn't remember having much. There was always food on the table but not a lot of luxury. At that time neighbors were very close. If her mother had extra milk, she'd give it to a family that had none. Those days were a pleasure to live through, yes sir. Yards so nice. She could always walk the shore in grassy spots and scoop up soft-shell crabs. A wilderness now, since Katrina.

Frank Campo played baseball with the Delacroix Island team. He shrimped after they married and she ran a country store with one gas pump and sold kerosene. Seems so far-fetched to think about now.

As far as she's concerned, women worked harder than the men in those days. Some of them on a boat, some of them at home. Wherever they were, they could handle anything. She woke up at three, four in the morning and with her husband rented out boats to sportfishermen and sold bait.

Dean Blanchard sits behind his desk and looks out the window at his silent dock on Grand Isle, a good three-hour drive from Shell Beach. Sure, he knows F.J. He's the one with the big marina, right? He knew Mr. Blackie better than F.J. Saw him on the TV. Anytime some reporter had a question about fishing, they called on Mr. Blackie.

Before the spill, Dean ran a full-service dock and processed a million pounds of mostly shrimp a year. Ninety-two percent shrimp, seven-and-a-half percent fish, he estimates. Something like that. Opened in 1972, surrounded by eight much larger competitors. He was the family-owned store next to a Walmart. He stood up to those Goliaths for twenty-eight years and drove each one out of business. Now, how many years later and he's how old? Fifty-fucking-one. By this time he'd planned to reap the rewards of a lifetime of work and retire.

Shit.

He unfurls a spreadsheet. Last year between July 1 and July 12, he sold $1.6 million of shrimp. This year for the same period and after all the closures, he sold just $241,658.47.

That's a big difference, he says.

Look here. This ice machine. Cost half a million dollars. Last year for those same dates, he sold $15.2 million of ice. This year for that same period, just $231.00. The goddamn ice machine's electric bill is $10,000 a day. You do the math.

He had ninety employees but has laid off all but eight or nine. That number's fixing to go down even more.

We're fucked, he says.

His momma's side of the family was in the oil business. His daddy was in oil. He knows how these people operate. Jesus hung around with fishermen, he didn't hang out with no oilmen.

There's a reason, Dean says.

The shrimp boats and oyster boats stand idle in their docks rocked softly by rolling waves. Seagulls float on unseen currents but soon disperse. Absent from the boats is the smell of fish, the chattering of men, the boastful stories. A silence fills the evening as the light fades to dark. Rain falls but has nothing to wash away. It pours off gutters and gathers in little pools beneath homes raised on stilts. Camps, people around here call these summer homes. Owned by sportfishermen from other parts of the state, other parts of the country. Not here. Not this summer.

Alton Blappert wanders onto his porch and considers a dense row of trees behind his property. Coyotes. That's where they come from, those woods there. He raises the .270 caliber, sights it at nothing, fires. Just to let them know he knows they are there.

Alton says:

It's not a business. It's a way of life out here.

I remember when corn, apples, and grapes grew right by shore. Big old mess of white clamshells on land. You could lay on them and they would be cool on top.

You've lived too long.

If my daddy came back he wouldn't want to live here.

My daddy bought the first automobile here. 1948. Took five hours to drive from here to Arabi. You had to stop and change tires. Five or six flats at least because of all the shells.

What place had the ice cream?

Rexall.

No, the Four Stop.

Root beer float.

Frozen mug.

The first trawl came from Biloxi in 1946, '47. The guy who

had it attached it to his cabin and pulled the goddamn cabin right off.

Who was that guy with the big suitcase and police dog?

He bought muskrat furs. Six dollars apiece. My uncle Pasqual took all his money and bought a house.

In those days, you get fifty, sixty baskets of crabs and you could be home by ten o'clock in the morning.

Set your line right. You tie your bait every six feet. Slipknot. Hold your line back and get the slack out of it. Crabs stayed on the bait as you pulled the line up. Scoop them in with a net.

That's right.

Traps licked that. Don't have to work at it now. They're in the traps.

Different caliber of fishermen then.

You've lived too long.

George Barasich sees the problem this way. The longer this oil lasts, the longer fishermen will work for BP. They might like it. They might not return to fishing even if they can. As the older guys leave, who trains the younger ones to fish?

He thinks of his father, how the old man watched him set nets, pick up the trawl, sort shrimp and throw what wasn't marketable overboard.

His old man was born in Croatia and followed his father to Biloxi when he was eleven. Then George's grandfather decided to return to the old country. His father stayed. There was nothing for him in Croatia. No such thing as foster care in those days. Fishermen raised him.

The old man lost his legs to diabetes. George called him Captain Bligh when he was fitted for prosthetic legs. He got around. He was seventy-three when he died. Fished until he was sixty-seven. Fought his legs a long time. Daylight to dark. You're slowing down, boy, he'd say. Pick up those shrimp. He had a lot of expectations and never offered a compliment. But if George did something wrong, the old man would be on him. He made a man of George, yes sir.

George made his kids work too. The oldest son is an electrical engineer. Another son is enrolled at Vanderbilt University. His sixteen-year-old daughter attends a private high school in Baton Rouge. Nine grand a year. Before the spill, all George did was work.

Folks here use hurricanes to measure time. Back in the day, they might say, Was that before Hurricane Betsy or after? Then Hurricane Katrina struck and blew Betsy permanently into the past. Now it's "before the spill" and "after the spill." Who would have thought anything would have been bigger than Katrina?

Katrina wiped out the Campo marina. Nothing left but space and wind and angry water. The fuel tanks lay in the few woods left standing. F.J. set them on blocks and washed them out. An EPA suit asked him what did he think he was doing. Don't take a fucking genius, F.J. told him. I'm washing my fuel tanks.

That's not legal, the EPA guy said.

Tell you what, F.J. told him. Why don't you get out? We've lost everything and you talk about legal, you motherfucker. He was hot, tired, sweating, and cleaning a six-thousand-gallon fuel tank. The parish sheriff, district attorney, some judges and state senators all bought their bait from the Campo marina. Who did this guy think he was?

Before you get too stupid I'll pull strings you've never seen, F.J. said. Get your ass out. I'm the king here.

I was in my uncle's arms in a trawl boat when I was eight months old. In diapers. How coon-ass is that?

You want to know how coon-ass my husband is? He was conceived on a reef.

Well, it was probably cold out and his momma needed some warming up.

The tides were right.

Strong currents.

Shrimp not the only ones feeding off the bottom.

Okay, it was supposed to go like this here. Janet Woodward lives in Arabi and had a friend there too named Steve. Steve knew a guy on a shrimp boat in Shell Beach. This guy bought his fuel from some guy named Campo and then he trawled for shrimp. Janet and Steve bought, say, 370 pounds of shrimp from this guy, and brought it to Steve's house. Pulled the heads off and put the shrimp in the freezer. Made five hundred bucks in sales. Whoever called, they wrote down their info, shipped them the shrimp. Cash only.

Janet passed out little business cards to get the word out. Crawfish too. Thirty to forty sacks. She went to bars around St. Bernard Parish. Bikers' night alone she'd sell $400 to $500 worth of crawfish.

One problem. The spill. Janet and Steve started their enterprise two weeks after the Deepwater well blew. She didn't think nothing of it. There had been spills before, there'd be spills again. Then the guy Steve knew on the shrimp boat texted him. Shrimp and crawfish areas closed down. Oh well, Janet thought, there goes another job. She had been unemployed for months before she and Steve hit on their plan. She made do cleaning houses but only just. Hiring herself out, not making much. Volunteered at a community center for the free food.

Oh well. Look at Pennsylvania and Ohio when steel crapped out. Everybody got screwed. We're not alone.

Dean Blanchard hears stories, conspiracy theories. Like who-really-killed-JFK kinds of stories. But these stories are all about BP. A lot of people are talking. Saying things like the contractors BP has hired to do the cleanup are directing shrimp boats away from the oil so it comes in on the beaches and they make more money because it will take more time to clean. Fishermen have told him that if you call in oil at certain coordinates the guy on the other end says, Don't tell nobody. Go ten miles the other way. When you don't see nothing, throw anchor.

Dean doesn't know the truth from the lies. He's just saying. It's what he's heard. He blames George Washington. Should have killed all the British when he had the chance.

At night Dean hears airplanes and helicopters fly overhead. Next day, oil in the water he saw with his own eyes is gone. Disbursements? What else? Guess what, they can't find oil for two weeks. Then it comes back. More billable hours.

He's just saying.

BP hired him to haul oil barges. But then they took that job away from him. Asked some other group to do it. Dean raised hell about it this morning. Cursed out the mayor. He told him, You want my two dogs? Well, one died. I'll bring you my last dog and my wife, how's that? You've taken everything else from me.

As soon as she heard the news and saw oil gushing out of the Deepwater well on TV, Mabel Campo knew they were in trouble. Oh my God, she says, I'm almost happy Frank's not here. He would be out of his mind. He was the kind of man where everything had to be just so with him. No in-between. A good old honest person.

If the spill kills oysters, that'll be trouble. Oysters won't come back like fish. They can't move, can't get away. Hurricanes are bad but the Campos always survived them. Most of these old fishermen she knows can't read or write. What other work can they do?

Shell Beach has lost homes and lives but it has always come back. She won't live anywhere else. She stayed in Baton Rouge with nine cousins for a while. She was so happy to return to Shell Beach. Baton Rouge was quiet. No noise just like here, but it was still different and not to her liking, no sir.

She knows F.J. hates waiting to be reimbursed by BP. The family can't keep charging stuff. They have never owed so much. Now she waits until he gets his BP check. Makes her nervous. Not used to operating like this, no sir.

She sees the stress in her friends. Nervous. Fear of the future. They say, What's it going to be like when this is over?

A friend had a heart attack. She knew he would. Saw it coming in his face. He's out of the hospital now, but she doesn't know how he's making out.

George Barasich keeps his 1973 wood and fiberglass shrimp boat at the Industrial Canal dock in New Orleans. It leaks a bit but nothing worth writing home about. The guy who owned it before George had abandoned it and it sat in the shipyard for thirteen months until George bought it for real cheap. He spent thirty grand fixing it to where he could put it back in the water. It was well worth it. He was anticipating a good shrimping season until the oil spill. He thinks it would be a good boat to get on BP's cleanup list. It would hold a bunch of people. Two in front, eight in the cabin. It has a lot of fuel capacity and could stay out a long time. Skim oil, haul boom, whatever. George would be captain. He would at least be that much but not a lick more.

F.J. sits in his boat in the middle of Lake Borgne. Waves roll against it like a dog licking his hand. He tastes salt and the freshness of the blue space around him. Seagulls soar, the sun barely up, the air still cool. The boat dips and rises in subtle swells. He and his grandson don't talk. Only a breeze whispers in his ears, leaving his mind a peaceful blank.

He is chasing something he can't see beneath the dark, brooding waters bonded together with that something by generations of fishermen who did the same thing and whose blood he carries and whose faces other than his daddy's and granddaddy's he knows only through old photographs and stories. He assumes it will be this way tomorrow and the next day and the day after that, until he too is a framed photograph in the hands of a great-great-grandchild who will know only his picture and the stories told about him when he was king.

He cherishes those times.

The Life Sentence of
Dicky Joe Jackson and His Family

As I sit in my car outside the medium-security federal prison in Forrest City, Arkansas, I clean my fingers.

"Before you get here, stop and buy you some of those hand wipes with bleach, and the last thing you do before you walk in is wipe your hands real good," inmate Dicky Joe Jackson had emailed me. "They use an ion spectrometer and nearly all money you touch out there has some trace of drugs on it, and it's their 'catch-all' device to deny you entry."

Contact with drugs from a used twenty-dollar bill is just one challenge facing me. Citing "safety and security concerns," prison administrators denied my request to interview Dicky, who insists I call him Joe. Although I am permitted to see him as a regular visitor, I cannot bring a pen, notepad, or recorder inside. After we meet I will go to my car and write down as much as I remember of our conversation. Not ideal for a reporter, certainly, but I have a backup plan. Before my visit Joe agreed to answer questions through the mail. I've already received several long, detailed letters from him describing his life and what led him to prison.

I throw the hand wipes onto the passenger seat, get out of my car, and squint against the steady gray drizzle this January morning. Because I can't take notes, the main purpose of my visit will be to put a face to Dicky Joe Jackson, a name I had come across a few weeks earlier in an ACLU report, *A Living Death*. The report summarized dozens of cases of the more than 3,200 men and women, including Jackson, serving life sentences without parole for nonviolent offenses.

In 1996, a federal court in Fort Worth found Joe guilty of conspiracy to possess with intent to distribute methamphetamine, possession with intent to distribute methamphetamine, being a felon in possession of a firearm, and possession of an unregistered firearm.

Joe, from the rural North Texas town of Boyd, needed thousands of dollars to pay for his critically ill son's monthly medical expenses. Transporting meth seemed the only way to do it. He thought he had known all the risks involved, but he hadn't. He didn't know he'd get busted. He didn't know he would stand in the courtroom of a judge who would show him no mercy. He didn't know that the man who supplied the meth, a man Joe had known for much of his life and considered a friend, would turn on him. And he didn't know that his wife would be left without a husband and his children without a father.

"I'm not making no excuses for what I've done," Joe told the judge at his sentencing hearing. "But when my son got sick, we tried every government agency there is to come up with the money, and nobody wanted to help us. And I don't expect you to help us now, neither."

The judge sentenced Joe to life.

Among those advocating for Joe's release is the man who prosecuted him, former assistant U.S. attorney Michael Snipes. He told me that nothing about his case indicated that he had committed or would commit a violent act.

"[Joe] potentially did this because he didn't know of any other way to take care of his kid," Snipes said. "As a prosecutor, I can say, 'Life, life, life,' but we're supposed to seek justice."

December 26, 2013

So, to answer your question, as far as where did I grow up, from birth till nine, I guess on the farm in Keeter [near Boyd]. From nine to seventeen we lived in Bridgeport and then moved back to the farm. But for real, I grew up in the cab of that Peterbilt [truck], all over the U.S. & Canada. As for favorite childhood memories, all on the farm before Dad got remarried & every visit to my Granny's house. And every trip I made with my Dad. As for values, do unto others as you'd have them do unto you but always remember, blood is thicker than water.

Sue Barrow sits in a booth at the back of a convenience store and restaurant off Texas State Highway 114 outside Boyd, about a ten-minute drive from the Jackson home. Seventy-five years old, worry lacing her soft country-accented speaking voice, she folds her small hands on the table and glances around, hoping the server doesn't object that she won't be ordering food. She'd just rather talk about her son, Joe Jackson. He was just two years old when she left him with his father, Billy Allen Jackson, a truck driver. It was an I'm-pregnant-let's-get-married sort of thing. She was nineteen, Billy Allen not much older. Stupid kids, she says. It didn't work out. Barrow then married an alcoholic who put a gun to the infant Joe's head, so Barrow gave him to Billy Allen to raise. Had Joe's youngest, Cole, been born healthy, Joe would never have done what he did, Barrow says. Cole got sick and then Billy Allen died of a heart attack and Joe had to look after his stepmother, too. He didn't know what he was going to do or where he would find the money.

"Look around," she says. "Nobody around here has a lot of money. They all just make a living."

I do look around. Highway 114 cuts through the center of Boyd, population 1,350, average yearly income about $15,000. The highway passes an assortment of small businesses—Hats Off Haircuts, Dandy Donuts—a library, and the Church of Christ. I can imagine flyers for Cole's fund-raisers taped to windows and telephone poles.

STREET DANCE & CRAFT BOOTHS
Saturday, April 11 noon
To benefit Joseph Cole Jackson
Bone Marrow Transplant Fund
Craft booth space $20 (all goes to fund)
Several bands to be featured

Sue's eyes tear up. She and every member of the family damn near begged for money to pay Cole's hospital bills. No one in their family had the kind of money the hospital was talking about. No, Joe didn't go to a bank. A man can borrow only so much, and if you don't have collateral, what bank is going to lend to you?

Sue shakes her head. She told Joe she knew how he was raising money for Cole. There was just too much coming in not to know.

"I can see what you're all fooling with and that's trouble," she told him. "I'm not some big ol' dummy. There's nothing worth your life."

But Joe wouldn't listen. He told her if he could save Cole's life, he'd gladly risk his.

When I leave the prison three hours later, I walk to my car at a fast clip just short of running. I keep repeating in my head the conversation I had with Joe, and when I reach my car I begin to write. Some of what he told me I knew from speaking with his family before my visit.

Joe wore wire-rimmed glasses, a white jumpsuit, and an easy smile. He had graying hair, a horseshoe-shaped mustache that framed his mouth, and a goatee. His voice had a southern lilt to it. A stocky man, he had the rolling walk of a sailor. He shook my hand and embraced me. We sat across from each other in a large room that reminded me of a school cafeteria. Shiny white tile floor, white and gray walls, and bright lights. Four other inmates sat across from their visitors. Sometimes, an inmate and their visitor would get up and stand in front of a painting of the Empire State Building and pose for photographs. Guards watched us talk, and in low voices we carved out our own space although we sat shoulder to shoulder with everyone else, and I asked my questions.

Joe told me he dropped out of high school at seventeen and began driving trucks and working alongside his father. He was twenty-seven when he bought his own eighteen-wheeler.

I recalled one of his letters. In it, he wrote that trucking had been his destiny. He'd been in and under trucks since grade school. He pulled his first transmission at thirteen. By the time he turned twenty, he knew more about trucks than some people twice his age.

A guard interrupted us and told Joe and the other prisoners to stand against a wall for a head count. The guard looked at them, checked a clipboard, looked at them again, and then told them to return to their seats, and Joe and I resumed talking.

Joe married his wife Yvonne in 1979 and they had three children, April, Jon, and Cole. Cole was born in 1990 with Wiskott-Aldrich syndrome, a rare and potentially life-threatening immunodeficiency disorder characterized by a reduced ability to form blood clots. It almost always affects boys. Treatments include bone marrow transplantation, transfusions of red blood cells, and the use of antibiotics. About the same time, the Jacksons lost their health insurance when an automatic deduction of the monthly premium did not clear the family's bank account. The Jacksons sued but the case dragged on for years.

Joe, who used small amounts of meth to stay awake when he drove across the country, said his supplier approached him about transporting the drug. The supplier said that if Joe agreed to take him to California, pick up a load of meth, and carry it into Texas, he would pay him $1,000 for every pound he carried. A typical haul would be about $5,000 to $11,000 worth of meth. The money would cover Cole's medical expenses, and Joe agreed.

Joe's uncle, Kenny Ludwick, played drums in country bands. He and his brother-in-law jammed at several fund-raisers for Cole. One time, they played a club in Newark, Texas, not that far from Boyd, right off Highway 287. If he had to go back, Kenny doubts it would still be there. When he considers those days, all he can say is that what happened to Cole, his illness and all, well, the family had never experienced anything like that with one of their children. Joe, he says, was looking for answers. He didn't whine. He was, Whatever it takes to save my boy, I'm going to do. Kenny didn't ask about Cole's medical bills, but he had an idea how Joe was paying them. How else could he get that kind of money? The Jacksons and their kin were just another close-knit family among many such families born and raised in and around Boyd, Kenny says. They didn't have shit in those days, but they didn't go hungry. They took care of their own, they took care of their kids.

Today, more than two decades later, Cole is a tall, lean twenty-three-year-old. He takes quite a few pills to boost his immune system. If he gets sick, it's not simple. A cold can last weeks, and there's always the worry that it could develop into something worse. He is alive, though, and mostly well. He has watched himself in family videos with his father. He doesn't know if he remembers those moments or just thinks he does because he has seen the videos so many times.

As a child, Cole never asked about his father. He didn't want to upset his mother. She was stressed enough struggling to support the family. They didn't go without, but they ate a lot of wieners, red beans, and potatoes. His mother didn't need him bothering her with questions. He learned about his father from stories he overheard. How his dad used to wrestle with April when she was little and call her "Bean" because she liked green beans. How Jon rode with him in his truck. It was like listening to stories about a dead person.

Cole understood from an early age that his father had done what he did for him. One time, when Cole was in Sunday school, the teacher read a piece of scripture that went something like this: The greatest deed a man can do is to give his life for his family. "That's my dad," Cole says. "He gave the ultimate."

From as far back as he can remember, Cole has carried a burden of guilt.

> *December 30, 2013*
> One day me & Dickie (that's my friend's name too, Dickie Spencer, and don't laugh, not everyone in Boyd is named Dickie, just me and him and his is "ie" instead of "y") are sitting in the office and Yvonne pulls in to get gas . . . So, I ask Dickie, who is that sweetheart there?

Yvonne Jackson no longer visits her husband. Ex-husband. They divorced, and she has not seen him since about 2001, but she does not think of him as her ex. Not yet, anyway, despite the passage of years. The divorce was his idea, Yvonne says. He wanted her to get on with her life. She has dated little. She doesn't know why, really. She just feels it's wrong that Joe's in there and she's out here. The divorce is not something she wants to remember. Several times she didn't show up at court. Then she told herself, "Get this divorce done." She thought it would be easier for him not to feel obligated to take care of her. She visited him after the divorce but it was too hard to see him. She figured it was better for both of them if she didn't go back.

They talk on the phone at least once a week, Sundays usually. "Get remarried yet?" he asks her. "Oh, shut up," she says. He asks about the kids and what they're doing. When they were younger, he always knew about their report cards. If they got in trouble at school or at home, he knew that, too. "When Dad calls, I'm going to tell him about what you did," Yvonne would say.

She grew up in Austin and moved to Boyd when she was in the eighth grade. Little bitty town then. Still is, though it has a Sonic now. That's new. She didn't think she would stay and then she met Joe. She was seventeen and saw him working in a gas station. He seemed nice. Quiet, shy, and calm. She let the air out of one of her tires and got him to fill it.

She returned later that week.

"Hey, dude," she said. "I'm skipping school. Want to skip with me?"

"I can't," Joe said. "I'm working. But after work I'll take you to a movie."

He had to get up early the next morning to help his father with a truck, so he and Yvonne ate at a McDonald's instead.

When Yvonne graduated from high school they married. Joe saved his money, bought her a ring. Got on one knee and proposed, the whole bit. He passed out when a nurse drew his blood for the marriage license. Joe, Yvonne learned, was afraid of needles.

They started their married life in a trailer home. Joe drove trucks, Yvonne worked at Burger Hut. In 1988 an undercover informant posing as a trucker at a Florida truck stop asked Joe if he had some speed. Joe gave him a pill. He was charged and convicted of possession of one-half gram of methamphetamine. He was given probation.

The Florida bust did not surprise Yvonne. She knew a lot of truckers took speed to stay awake. When someone says, "We need a load in California," and you're not getting enough hours to make a living, you do what you have to do to stay awake and haul your load.

One month, when Joe and Yvonne borrowed money for two weeks to pay for diapers, Joe told her, "We'll never do this again. And you know what? We're going to have a house. We need a house. I grew up in a trailer. My kids won't."

Soon after, Yvonne said, they built a log cabin on ten acres. Joe earned just $20,000 a year. How could they afford a house and land, Yvonne wondered, but she didn't ask questions. Joe brought the check home like everybody else.

The cabin had almost been completed when police arrested Joe in Tylertown, Mississippi, in December 1989 for carrying more than a kilogram of marijuana in his truck. He called Yvonne and said, "I've got bad news." She understood then where the money for the cabin had come from. He was sentenced to twelve months.

"I think Joe never felt good enough," Yvonne told me. "My mother didn't like him. 'He's a truck driver,' she'd say. Maybe he thought if he gave us all this stuff, did all these things for us, we'd love him. He never thought he was giving us enough."

While Joe was locked up, Yvonne gave birth to Cole.

January 5, 2014

While I was down there [in the Tylertown jail], Cole was born and I knew God was sending me a message—all that illegal money you made was dust in the wind. So, when we found out he needed the [bone marrow] transplant, our insurance skipped, it was gonna cost $250,000 and we needed half to get him admitted [to the hospital], and the fact we only had 2 years to do this in order to save him, we still kept our cools & put our trust in God instead of Joe [me]. But the problem was, I'd done found out I more or less had the key to Pandora's box if you will. I had a truck & knew if nothing else worked, I'd haul something illegal & get the money. That thought always riding there in my pea-sized brain corrupted my faith or it was just weak anyway, I don't know, probably both.

Joe's marijuana arrest had surprised his stepmother, Juanita Jackson. Then again, because she was a trucker too and worked almost every day, she didn't see him all that often and had no idea what he might be up to. Joe didn't talk to her about a whole lot of stuff. Juanita had married Joe's father, Billy Allen Jackson, when Joe was three. Joe was one of those boys who didn't need to work hard to keep his grades up. He could draw too, trucks mostly. Trucks were his life, just as they were for his father. Juanita knew Billy took speed to stay awake driving. Not often—he didn't usually have to drive but eight hours on any given job.

One morning, Juanita remembers, Yvonne drove to her house with Cole, who was just weeks old. He had red spots all over him. Juanita had had rashes growing up but she'd never seen anything like this.

Neither had Yvonne. She asked a friend, "What's this on Cole? Heat rash?" And, like Juanita, her friend said, "I don't think so." Yvonne called Cole's pediatrician in Fort Worth. "Something's wrong with Cole," she told a nurse. "I need to bring him in."

Cole's doctor referred him to a hospital for a blood test. When the results came in, a nurse told Yvonne that Cole's platelet count was very low. Platelets help the body clot blood.

"Call your family," the nurse said. "Cole is really sick."

Yvonne telephoned her mother and Billy Allen and Juanita.

"Something's wrong with the baby," she said.

When Joe finished his sentence, in December 1990, Yvonne brought Cole with her when she picked him up. Joe got in the truck and Yvonne started crying. "The baby's real sick, Joe," she said.

"Why didn't you tell me?"

"Because you had to stay here."

"What if he'd died?"

"Well, he's been going to the hospital."

In 1991, the Jacksons sold everything they didn't need—trailers, trucks, tools—to pay for Cole's bone marrow transplant. They arranged fund-raisers and asked a Sunday school teacher to supervise the effort.

Yvonne and Joe wrote to everyone they could think of for items to auction. They set up garage sales and sent letters to the Dallas Cowboys asking for donations. Different vendors arranged events for Cole. Bowl for Cole. Bake sale for Cole. Rodeo for Cole. Posters for fund-raisers with a photograph of Cole plastered telephone poles and the windows of local businesses.

The family raised $50,000 in twelve months. A Chicago nonprofit matched the amount and the hospital agreed to perform the transplant, but the family was still obligated to pay the difference of about $150,000.

The bone marrow of eleven-year-old April was a perfect match for Cole.

"You'll be saving Cole's life," her parents told her. "It's important you do this."

April was scared but moved to know she would be helping

Cole. She remembers a long needle inserted into her hip to draw some of her bone marrow. She was given an anesthetic but it still hurt to walk afterward.

Cole lived in the hospital's transplant unit from June to September 1992. Antibiotics were injected into a catheter in his chest that led directly to his heart. His parents had to scrub down and wear hospital gowns before they could visit with him. April and Jon pressed a button and spoke to him through glass. For his second birthday, they held his presents up to the window. Four boys shared the unit with him. They all had cancer and had died by the time the hospital discharged Cole.

Cole thinks he remembers the morning he left but probably not because he was only two. April told him he didn't want to leave. The hospital had been home for a long time.

But the transplant did not fully reverse the syndrome. Doctors put him on the drug Gammagard to help fight infection. It cost about $3,700 a month, Yvonne says. Cole also required weekly blood tests that cost $400 each. In addition, the family had prescriptions to fill. Dozens of medicine bottles cluttered the kitchen counter. Yvonne remembers one cost $250 for each refill.

Joe thought the doctors were crazy. He just wanted to fix Cole.

"You take care of him," Joe told Yvonne. "I'll take care of everything else."

During my prison visit, Joe told me he began hauling meth after his father died in October 1993 and he assumed his stepmother's mortgage payment and other expenses. Up until then, Jackson had been scraping by paying Cole's medical bills, but this new obligation overwhelmed him. He enlisted his brother Tommy to drive the supplier when he couldn't.

Yvonne knew what he was up to. She knew that some of the people he hung around with weren't nice. She knew, too, that if they didn't have money to pay for Cole, he would die. She understood the money Joe brought home did not come from the generosity of strangers.

"We talked about it," Joe wrote to me. "I mean, how could we not? Yvonne was terrified & of course all I could do was lie to her and tell her it would all work out. She knew in her heart I was gone & she would be left to pick up & carry on all by herself."

> *February 18, 2014*
> Believe me, after just doing a year in Mississippi, the farthest thing [from] my mind was having to do something illegal again. I ran both my trucks as hard & fast as I could for a year & then sold them both. I done everything I could and done it all legal and probably never would have gotten into any more trouble if that transplant would have done what they said & healed my son. I would have been happy working in that shop doing paint & body & never leaving home. It just didn't turn out like that.

In May 1995, federal agents raided Joe's home and the homes of Juanita Jackson and his brother Tommy. Juanita was still in bed when they showed up at five, maybe six in the morning. She opened the front door to ten or more plainclothes officers.

"Do you have weapons?" one of them demanded.

She was so shocked she could barely answer. "Yes, a gun. A deer rifle. It's never been used. I'll get it."

"No, ma'am. We will," an officer told her. They stayed a long time. Juanita gathered from the way they talked that they were looking for drugs. They didn't find anything other than her medication.

About the same time federal agents knocked on Juanita's door, Yvonne woke to an odd sound. Joe was in Arizona delivering a load of Gatorade. She looked out a window and saw helicopters and a plane and dozens of men in camouflage fatigues. One of them spoke into a loudspeaker: "Come out with your hands up!"

Yvonne put her three children in a bedroom. She knew someone had made a huge mistake. It's the neighbor they want, she thought. The police had been at his house several times before. She walked outside and dots from the agents' laser sites covered her body. One of them told her to quiet her Rottweiler, Die Hard, or he'd shoot it. He then asked her name and if anyone else was inside. After she answered, he asked if the children belonged to Joe Jackson.

"Yes," Yvonne said. "All I have in the house is my three kids. I'm going back in there."

The agents asked her to bring the children out onto the porch. After a while, they told her to leave while they searched the house. She made Jon go to school. She thought if they did normal things, they would all wake up and everything would be just as before. Yvonne took April and Cole to her mother's house. Four hours later, she returned to her home. It looked as if a tornado had blasted through. Pots and pans all over the place. Couches overturned. A computer broken. Clothes thrown every which way on the floor. All the loose change had been taken. A paper thing Jon had made in school was torn up, and the baby books too. Yvonne's lingerie was strewn across the bed.

No drugs were found in the house and no warrant was issued for Joe, but Yvonne knew it was only a matter of time. She called him in Arizona. "The feds are looking for you," she said. No one at Jon's school knew about the raid. Eight-year-old Jon felt weird not talking about it. It was the same kind of feeling he got when his grandfather Billy Allen died. Just weird.

Jon remembers his mother and father talking. He felt the tension between them. Seemed like they were both worried. Real worried. They knew there would be trouble. "I may do some time," his father said. Joe returned home from Arizona only to find that the authorities had not yet issued a warrant for his arrest. He continued working. He had bills to pay and a son who was still sick. He didn't haul much meth after the May raid; he knew the end was near.

In November, Joe's house was raided again and a warrant issued for his arrest. He was not home at the time, but on the advice of an attorney he turned himself in. By then Tommy had been arrested in California and extradited to Texas. Both brothers refused to cooperate with Michael Snipes, the assistant U.S. attorney, and testify against the supplier. The supplier, however, had other ideas. He testified against Joe, and accused him of being the ringleader. According to transcripts, the supplier said that between the spring of 1993 and October 1994, he and Joe drove to California "eight or nine" times and bought "probably 180 pounds" of meth. Joe disputed the amount when I spoke to him in prison. He said he had transported five to eleven pounds of meth two times from October to December 1993 and three or four times from January 1994 to May 1995.

The supplier had taken the stand before Judge John McBryde. McBryde is known in Texas for his harsh sentencing. In 1997, one year after Joe's trial, the Fifth U.S. Circuit Court of Appeals issued a rare public reprimand, finding McBryde to have "abused judicial power, imposed unwarranted sanctions on lawyers, and repeatedly and unjustifiably attacked individual lawyers and groups of lawyers and court personnel." His "intemperate, abusive and intimidating treatment of lawyers, fellow judges, and others has detrimentally affected the effective administration of justice and the business of the courts in the Northern District of Texas."

McBryde was not allowed any new cases for a year. He denied the circuit court's characterizations of his behavior. But "he's known for not giving insignificant sentences," said Texas criminal law attorney William S. Harris. "He is unashamed of his relatively conservative and severe sentencing. That's a fair statement and one I think he wouldn't disagree with." McBryde's office did not return my calls.

Believing that his attorney was charging too much and doing too little, Joe hired another lawyer, Bill Lane. But Lane was unable to prevent the jury from delivering a guilty verdict on February 14, 1996. McBryde would determine the sentence at a hearing later that spring.

On May 17, 1996, Lane spoke before McBryde of Joe's "gravely ill son." He suggested federal sentencing guidelines offered some leeway, "departing downward when we have an individual that's faced with a situation of duress."

Lane then submitted to the court a folder of forty letters from family, friends, and the community requesting leniency for Joe. Another folder contained photographs, letters, and medical reports concerning Cole.

According to the transcripts, McBryde said he had "read all the letters, and I was very impressed with the letters."

"I'd ask the court to take that into consideration and give Joe Jackson whatever consideration you can," Lane said, "as much as it's clear throughout that two-volume [set of letters and doctors' reports] the situation that this family was in. And I'm not sure, being a father of four small children myself, I'm not sure what situation I would find myself in with a life-threatening situation with a young child and nowhere to turn; and flatly, Judge, several doctors and hospitals saying, 'If you don't come up with the cash, we're not going to save your child.'"

Lane sat down. The courtroom grew quiet. The Jackson family watched McBryde. He didn't speak right away. Jon thought McBryde looked huge in his black robe and he started to cry.

> The Court: OK. The court orders, adjudges and decrees that the defendant be committed to the U.S. Bureau of Prisons to serve a term of imprisonment of life—
>
> Mrs. Jackson: No, no, no.
>
> The Court: —on each of the Counts 1, 6, and 7 of the indictment.
>
> Mrs. Jackson: No. No. You can't do that. You can't just take him away. No, no. You're not God. You're not.
>
> (Mrs. Jackson leaves the courtroom.)

Although he had no prior convictions, Tommy Jackson also received a life sentence. The supplier was sentenced to ten years.

February 18, 2014

As for going back to jail after sentencing, they put us in the hole. Said we'd be a danger to the general population and we can't have that but promised us they would try & get us on to prison as soon as possible. And they did. Exactly one month later, we were on a bus headed to the Federal Transfer Center at Oklahoma City. Tommy was going to Florence [Colorado], & I was headed to Leavenworth [Kansas].

Bill Lane told me that Joe "did a stupid and criminal act but he's not a criminal. He didn't get up every morning to rob somebody. His mind-set was to take care of his kid. I've had the pleasure of representing real criminals. They accept the risk. Jail is part of doing business. That wasn't his deal. He had a reason. It's not legal justification to do what he did. It doesn't limit his culpability but it does allow for giving him some slack."

Michael Snipes said he has always had "a bad feeling" about Joe's case. Snipes, now a judge, insisted that he had no quarrel with the life sentence; that was what federal sentencing guidelines called for at the time. However, though the guidelines made the sentence "fairly mandatory," McBryde "still could have departed down if he wished. He didn't necessarily have to do it."

In 2013, Snipes wrote a letter on behalf of Joe in support of the family's effort to obtain clemency or a pardon. "I prosecuted hundreds, if not thousands, of cases during my thirteen-year career with the United States Attorney's Office," Snipes wrote. "I saw no indication that Mr. Jackson was violent, that he was any sort of large-scale narcotics trafficker or that he committed his crimes for any reason other than to get money for his gravely ill child. Although I have no personal knowledge of how Mr. Jackson has performed as an inmate, I would support any decision to pardon or give him clemency based on the facts of the case."

I told Snipes that his support of Joe surprised me. I'd read the trial transcripts and saw no hint of his conflicted feelings. "I was doing my job," Snipes said.

> *January 21, 2014*
> It's already Saturday, you're off visiting my family in [Texas] and I'm probably one of the loneliest people in the country right now. You asked me to describe my life in prison and that's the best description there is—lonely . . . I'd just as soon every day be Monday. And I try to make 'em all Monday too. I try to find something to keep me busy every day, all day. If you ever stop moving in here, it all comes rushing back at you—home & how you miss it.

Sue Barrow has never visited Joe in Forrest City. Too long a drive for an elderly person, she says. But she thinks of him every day. She remembers going to the hospital and seeing him with Cole. He would stay half the day with him and Yvonne the other half.

Sue has written more senators than she can name about Joe's situation but they don't have time to fool with her. If you do the crime, you do the time. That's a response she has received two or three times. She blames herself for Joe's incarceration. She should have been a better mother instead of screwing around when she was younger. "I'm paying for it now," she says. "I'm paying for my son in the worst possible way."

Juanita Jackson doesn't dwell too much on what people say about Joe. He did for Cole what he knew to do. Trucking and hauling. That's all he knew. That's how he dealt with it. She visited him in prison in Leavenworth and Beaumont, Texas. El Reno, Oklahoma, too. Drove there by herself, an hour or so. Hasn't been to Forrest City. She had knee replacement surgery last year and can't sit in a car too long. Joe called the other day. She told him the electricity that pumped water from her well had played out. It had been fixing to do that for a while. She called a well man and an electrician. Wasn't cheap. "Well, Mom," Joe said, "if you had told me there was a problem, I'd've fixed it before I come to jail."

April needed someone to blame after her father was sentenced. Just fourteen years old at the time, she fought a lot with her mother. "Why didn't you stop it?" she'd say. "Why didn't you stop him from doing it?" Sometimes she spoke to her father as if he could hear her. "Why'd you do this? I need you."

She grew to hate Boyd. Such a small town. People would ask her, How's your dad? He's incarcerated, isn't he? She wanted to punch them. Vicious gossips. She felt people were watching her. After high school, she wanted to get out of Boyd. She attended Texas Christian University for one year and then drove to South Padre Island for the summer and decided to stay, forfeiting her scholarship. Later she lived in Brownsville, dated, and became pregnant. She worried that her father would be disappointed in her. They spoke every week by phone, and he comforted her. "I'm in prison," he told her. "How can I be disappointed in you?"

April is thirty-two now and married. She and her brother Jon co-own a custom design printshop. Cole works there too. In January she had her fourth child, a boy. Until his birth, she and her brothers and her older children had visited Joe regularly. The children, April says, have grown close to their grandfather. He talks to them on the phone and sends cards on their birthdays. They know he is in prison for drugs. They know he won't get out. They ask their mother, How does he buy groceries? Where does he eat?

April remembers the good times. Those times when she was little and she'd ride with her father in his truck. She'd sit up front, her mother in back. She and her father sang songs. She liked how the purple lights on the sides of the truck would light up snow at night. "The only memories we have in the last eighteen years are those sitting in a prison visiting room," she says. Sometimes she wonders if her father would have been better off had he received the death penalty. It feels selfish to hope nothing happens to him, yet it would be easier for him if something did. She would grieve and then the healing would begin. There's no healing with a life sentence, only limbo and constant worry.

He did what he did, and April is glad he was caught and punished and has learned that what he did was wrong. But he wasn't there to walk her down the aisle, see the birth of her children. Does the punishment fit the crime? She doesn't think so and feels cheated by the years without him. You can be dead set against something like drugs until something happens to you, she says, and then it's hard to know how you'd react or where you'd turn for help. Maybe she'd have a different outlook if she wasn't in this situation. But she is.

As a boy, Jon could not comprehend life without his father. He made up stories. He'd say his father was on a truck driving to Maine, the farthest place he could think of to explain his father's absence. When he turned twelve, Jon started working in a cabinet shop. By then he had stopped telling people his father was in Maine. His friends didn't come over as much, but he didn't care. He didn't need people around. Now, at twenty-six, he still doesn't. He and his father are just alike. Jon knows everything about cars and trucks. They talk about new trucks over the phone, though the conversations aren't easy. Fuel-injected engines weren't in widespread use when his father went to prison. It took Jon six months to help his father understand some of the vehicles coming out. He sent him photographs and they went over them on the phone.

Jon doesn't like to think of his parents' divorce. His mother told him and he got upset, but after a while he understood. You can't have a marriage with someone locked up. He'd bring up the divorce just to be a bad kid. "You left Dad, I don't need to listen to you," he'd tell his mother. One day his father called from prison and said something about a man Yvonne was dating. "I guess Mom's boyfriend is a good guy," he told Jon. "I guess you got a new dad." Jon went off. To him, it wasn't like that. To him, his father was his father and no one else. No one.

"You're not here, Dad," Jon snapped. "You ain't got no right to say that to me."

Silence. Then his father started crying.

Cole and his friends were so young when his father went to jail that none of them understood what had happened and no one sassed Cole about it. Instead, everyone was on him to be careful, but sometimes he didn't listen. Like this one afternoon. He was about six years old and still seeing doctors at least twice a week. He jumped his bicycle over a cinder block, fell, and cut his left shin. He bandaged it and continued playing. He woke up in the middle of the night and his bedsheets were covered with blood. The cut hadn't clotted. His mother rushed him to the hospital. He understood then that his illness prevented him from playing games other boys played.

Although Cole got to know his father on prison visits, it was hard to talk to him with April and Jon and everybody else trying to talk to him too. In hindsight, he felt the journeys were sometimes more memorable than the visits. Cole can't count the number of times he watched a video of *The Fox and the Hound* on car trips. That ended on a drive to see Joe in Leavenworth, when someone broke into their Blazer overnight and stole the video and the portable TV/VCR he used to watch it.

At Leavenworth, Cole's father entertained him with card tricks he'd learned from another inmate. Illusions. They fooled Cole. His father always had a new magic trick. Another time, Cole's father had a beard and Cole didn't recognize him for a minute. His mother always went along on prison visits, until one day she didn't. "Me and Dad divorced," she said. It didn't change much. Cole's father had been gone awhile by then. It wasn't as if there'd been joint custody.

Little things determine whether you know somebody, Cole says. He knows his father likes rock 'n' roll, but if he and Cole went to a restaurant, Cole wouldn't know what his father would want to eat.

When he considers his life, Cole shrugs and figures that somehow he beat the odds and lived. His doctors don't know why. Maybe his illness will catch up to him like Parkinson's caught up with Muhammad Ali. Until then, he'll just keep doing what he's doing and not worry. He talks to his father once a week. His father is a good listener. Cole tells him things like he would a parent, yet his father doesn't seem like a parent. More like a relative he rarely sees. Joe may not be here with Cole, but Cole is convinced that he would not be here at all if it weren't for his father.

He thinks about his father the same way he considers history. Back during the Vietnam War, people called returning American soldiers "baby killers." They didn't know what they were talking about. They weren't in that situation. How could they judge? The same is true with his father. A big-money drug dealer was the only person he knew to go to for help. People say that he could have done this or that. Do they have sick kids? Do they have health insurance? Do they have good-paying jobs?

"Makes a difference," Cole says.

Joe has been in prison almost twenty years now, Yvonne Jackson thinks to herself. He was thirty-seven when he was sentenced, she was thirty-five. They didn't know it then, but they were just kids. Just two scared kids. Boyd filled with rumors after his arrest. People said the Jacksons had money stashed in tunnels under their house. Bodies lay buried on the property. When she attended one of April's basketball games, people sat away from her. She was kicked off the PTA and no longer allowed to substitute-teach. "My daddy didn't do drugs," she overheard April tell a girl one day. "He hauled them. Get it right."

A fire at a neighbor's house damaged the Jackson home, and the $8,000 Yvonne received from insurance helped pay Cole's bills. Then, after Joe had been imprisoned for about ten years, a lawyer called. He told her their former health insurer had agreed to pay a $5,000 penalty for having discontinued the family's health care coverage. Life didn't stop, however. There were so many bills. At one time, Yvonne worked three jobs. She also opened a restaurant with her mother, and since people enjoyed gossiping about the Jacksons, called it Talk of the Town.

She is employed today with a telecommunications company. She does not blame Joe for the difficult years. He did what he thought was best for his family. Guys are made to take care of their families, to provide for them, and that's what he did. While Cole was hospitalized, the father of one of the boys in his isolation unit abandoned his family, Yvonne recalls. He couldn't cope with the stress of his son's terminal cancer. But Joe never left. People can say what they want about him, but they better say that, too. Joe never left.

And the Walls Came Tumbling Down

Miami spoiled him. Denny's restaurant. Cracker Barrel Old Country Store. Three fried eggs, bacon, toast, and pancakes for breakfast. It had been weeks since Michael Brewer had eaten that well. Weeks since he had used a bathroom. He showered twice a day just because he could. And clean sheets on a bed. A real bed. He wrapped himself in the sheets and laughed.

Thoughts of Haiti, however, stayed with him. The boys. Like family. He has no other besides his eighty-year-old mother. No ties that bind him anywhere else. Michael, Michael, Michael, the boys chant, demanding his attention. You get to know these kids, it's pathetic, Michael tells friends. They're good kids, not bad. Good intellect. They have a hell of a lot of potential but are ignored.

In Miami he didn't see anyone. They were either in their houses or cars, A/C on, windows shut. It was weird. He was used to having the kids around.

He awoke one morning at four and remembered Emmanuel wanted boots. He got up, drove to a Walmart, and found a pair for nineteen bucks. A steal, even on his budget. Hours later, he caught a flight to Port-au-Prince.

Now he regrets leaving.

Michael stands, stoop-shouldered with a slight paunch, in the middle of a speck of dry, desolate land above Port-au-Prince that someone, he doesn't know who, dubbed Camp Benedictine. The humidity laces a cotton haze over the horizon. He downs a can of Battery, a local energy drink, and fingers his shirt pocket for a smoke. Flies dart around him. Men and women piss in the open outside makeshift shacks, an uneven, quilted patchwork of aluminum siding, cardboard, and blue tarps filled with what little clothing they have been able to collect. Children carry inflated condoms like balloons, while other kids make kites from discarded plastic bags. More homeless people gather at a well, all of them, Michael included, victims of the catastrophic January 12 7.0-magnitude earthquake that rocked Haiti and killed more than 200,000 men, women, and children. Buildings, too, fell by the thousands, including the four houses Michael had built for homeless kids when he started his nonprofit Haitian Street Kids Inc. in 2000. Three of his kids died when buildings collapsed on them.

The widespread destruction included all of Port-au-Prince hospitals; air, sea, and land transport facilities; and communication systems. Debris blocked shattered roads. People slept in the street, in their cars, or in temporary camps, fearful that damaged buildings would not withstand the steady wave of aftershocks that followed the earthquake.

Now, almost four months later, the rubble has been removed from the roads, aftershocks are few, and downtown Port-au-Prince bustles with traffic, but the ruin of people's lives remains visible in the hundreds of camps still standing and in the weary faces of homeless families waiting for the billions in promised international aid to filter down to them.

In March 2010, UNICEF promised Michael three large tents to use as a dormitory, a school, and a clinic. The Clinton Foundation promised him a truck. More than four weeks have passed. How much time does it take? If he's not a hundred years old by the time these promises are kept, he'll be all right. Communication is terrible. His laptop was stolen. *Vòlè* motherfuckers, he says, using the Creole word for "thief." He doesn't answer email as fast as he should, and that could cost him funders, cost the kids real shelter that keeps out the heat, wind, and rain.

After the earthquake, a prosthetic factory offered to hire some of his boys. Michael had it all planned and then never heard from the factory owner again. Construction jobs, the same thing. The kids get all wired up and then nothing happens. They look at Michael as though he failed them. But they stay. Street kids have nothing. They are not in the child welfare system because they have no adult to register them. Orphanages don't want street kids, and no family asks to adopt a fifteen- or sixteen-year-old kid. Michael had one orphanage director tell him there was no money in helping teenagers. Michael asked him, "What business are you in again?"

Mormons adopted two boys he knew. You can improve your life, they told him and the kids. He hated that. They assumed that his life needed changing. They knew nothing about him or his kids. They needed to get off their asses and do something, he thought. Well, they got off their asses and adopted two boys. Michael wasn't crazy about two of his kids living with Mormons, but at least they were in the U.S. now.

He needs money but he doesn't have a clue about getting corporate sponsors and endowments. He asks friends for donations and tries to attract media. With money, he could rent a house so he and the boys would no longer have to live in a camp. Yeah, a house. Where he and the boys can again take for granted running water and a working kitchen and clean bathrooms and hot showers and fans.

He's two years shy of sixty. I'm starting over, he reminds himself.

Michael was a registered nurse in the Department of Defense when he started helping homeless kids in Haiti. In 1999, he had two months off his medical reconnaissance missions and decided to visit Haiti and look into child slavery. At-risk kids had been the focus of his nursing studies. What he saw in Haiti was much worse than he'd expected. Kids chained to beds. Kids not allowed to eat more than one meal a day. Whipped. Beaten. Lemon juice dripped into their wounds. Worked like dogs. Treated worse than dogs.

He met kids who had escaped slavery and lived on the street. Young. Six, seven, eight, nine, ten years old, maybe. Most didn't know their ages. In the ghetto of Cité Soleil he found a five-year-old boy lying on rocks, naked, unconscious. He had been abandoned at the age of two because his family thought his epileptic seizures meant he was possessed by demons. He lived on garbage and handouts. Passersby placed bets on when he would die. Ti Zo, they called him, Creole for "little bones" or "little money."

Michael started CPR on the boy. Two quick breaths into his mouth and he got a pulse back. He picked him up. No, monsieur, the people warned him. Leave him. Michael carried him to Sisters of Charity Hospital and paid for three days of care. Then he found an orphanage, St. Joseph's Home for Boys. But when he returned for Ti Zo, the hospital had released him. Michael walked throughout Cité Soleil looking for him. In gutters, trash piles, abandoned houses. When he was about to give up, he turned a corner and saw Ti Zo standing by himself in a vacant alley in the shadow of a wall. Michael took him to the orphanage.

Next, he found three kids under a bridge. He fed them day by day. He rented a room with an outdoor shower and toilet and the room next to it. He put the kids in the rooms and hired a man to watch them.

He returned to the States and tacked a photo of the boys on his office wall. The kids never complained, just took their lumps. Unlike at his work, where people complained all the time—about the weather, lunch, their spouses. Then somebody said something that set him off, he doesn't remember what. Something insignificant. Something stupid. But it was enough for him to stand up and say, See you guys in another life. He resigned, jumped on a plane, and moved to Haiti. Rented a two-story house, collected more kids, and enrolled them in school. Must have had seventy kids at least, ages six to fifteen. Once he got started he couldn't stop, couldn't leave, couldn't abandon them. Who else would do it?

No matter what he thought about his former DOD coworkers, he could not escape the fact that he had learned his sense of right and wrong in a developed nation, and year after year for ten years those sensibilities informed his disgust with Haitians' seemingly cruel indifference to the suffering of children.

He stayed.

On January 9, 2010, Michael left Haiti for the first time in seven years to visit his home state of Texas and raise money for

Haitian Street Kids. The boys told him to enjoy himself. Eat well. Get fat. The earthquake struck three days later. News of it flashed on a television screen, and Michael freaked. There were no functioning telephone lines. No way to call his kids. He contacted television news stations and was interviewed about the earthquake and the plight of his kids. A nonprofit, Airline Ambassadors International, responded to the broadcasts by offering him a flight to Haiti.

The American military had taken over the Port-au-Prince airport. Haitians wandered the streets in shock. Like blind people, they bumped into one another and continued walking, dazed and lost. Michael saw hundreds of bodies massed on street corners, huge mounds of stiffened corpses. He covered his nose but the stench stayed with him.

His four two-story cinder-block homes had been reduced to rubble. One boy, Chelo, fourteen, did not get out of one of them before it collapsed on top of him. He had been sold into slavery by his mother. Michael had met him when he was getting water for his owner and convinced the child to come to his program. Chelo loved school. He was quiet. Never got pissed off. He enjoyed helping other street kids. A contractor told Michael that it would cost five thousand dollars to retrieve his body. Michael didn't see the point. There would be nothing left of Chelo to remove.

He searched for survivors and moved with them to the barren hilltop he now calls home. Families followed him and expected Michael to care for them as well. The girlfriends of some of his older boys also joined him. Michael, Michael, Michael, they say when they see him each morning. Michael, Michael, Michael. As if his name alone will solve everything.

Mwen grangou. I'm hungry.

I have no money, he says. I am buying food on credit. Then he digs into his pocket and doles out what little change he has.

Michael, Michael, Michael.

I want your shirt, a boy tells him.

I want your hat, Michael says.

Sometimes he gets so damn pissed he thinks he and all aid agencies should leave, screw Haiti. The kids drive him nuts. Petty jealousies, they want this or that, vie for his attention. They owe money. They want iPods—iPods! They have no business with iPods, Michael thinks. They accuse each other of stealing. It's always something. A Haitian teen version of the DOD.

But these are desperate kids, not spoiled adults. The problem is hormones and need. He's stuck with a bunch of adolescents with survival problems and kid problems all bundled together in one neurotic mess.

At night the shacks and even the people disappear into an impenetrable darkness. Voices rise and fall, dissociated from the mouths producing them. Pans clatter. Sandals flap against the stones. Cooking fires diminish to ash. Michael sits on a white plastic chair and holds a flashlight beneath his chin. He turns it on and makes faces at some children collected at his feet. They scream, delighted, and scamper off. He chases them. *Arrrrrrrr*, he growls. The children scream again and run around him. Some of the older boys join in and soon everyone is running in circles, even the barking dogs, chasing each other, laughing.

Seconds later, his mood shifts. Michael returns to his chair, cradles his chin in his hands. The children wait expectantly.

He looks at them, stares through them. Lights a cigarette. Brooding. How does he get them and himself off this hilltop?

In the morning, Michael awakens to the crowing of roosters. The sun is not yet up and the air retains the coolness of night. Men and women wander by him, balancing bundles of clothes on their heads. Dogs lounge on the cool ground. The gray sky stretches like a thin blanket overhead and grows paler as the sun rises, hinting of the heat to come in streaks of searing white light. Trucks rumble through the camp, churning up brown dust.

Slow down, dickweed! Michael shouts at the drivers.

He pours water from a plastic bottle into one hand and splashes his face and rubs vigorously. I've had my shower, he says, wiping his eyes. I'm John the Baptist. I wander Haiti, eat bugs. He tugs on a white T-shirt, a pair of jeans, and black boots. He doubles over, coughs a smoker's cough, and sounds like he will spit up a lung. Then he lights a cigarette. He hears someone shouting and sees a woman beating a boy with a stick. The boy covers his head and she grabs his arms and tries to bite his neck.

Jesus! Michael screams. Jesus Christ! What are you doing? You don't bite! Jesus! He pushes the woman away. She tries to get around him, waves the stick. He snatches it from her. She shouts louder, backs away. Some of the men watching laugh. Michael examines the boy's neck. Four holes. Like a fucking vampire. The woman told the boy to buy her something and he didn't want to, and that set her off, the boy tells him. That and the heat and living on a withered patch of land without shade and water.

The boy wanders off with other boys. The woman joins some women seated around a cooking fire, muttering fiercely to herself. Michael finishes his cigarette. The jolt of energy that issued from the woman's outrage dissipates into the rising waves of heat, the steady wailing of babies, the panting of dogs, and the realization that there is nothing else to do now but wait until the day ends with nightfall and sleep, and in those dispassionate hours when time passes rapidly and unnoticed, a new day begins gathering itself in the shadows to emerge finally at dawn as a force of heat and monotony. Another long, weary, aimless, hot morning when tempers simmer.

There is Kendy, twenty. He has been with Michael since he was ten. He has scrawled on his arms the names of the girls in his life: Kendy and Minion, Kendy and Monioniz, Kendy and Loulie, Kendy and Krystie, Kendy and Donnuela.

Michael found him outside a Port-au-Prince hospital. He had been struck by a taxi and suffered a compound fracture in his right leg. Some people picked him up and laid him down in front of the hospital. He stayed there three days. The broken bone pierced his skin, protruding from his leg. Passersby gave him food and water. He pissed in a bottle. His leg became infected. A doctor took him into the hospital, put a layer of cotton over the bone, and then wrapped his leg in plaster. By then, kids Michael was working with told him about Kendy. He drove to the hospital at eleven o'clock and found him outside its doors. The cast had turned yellow from infection. Michael took Kendy home and cut off the cast and cleaned the break. It took three months for Kendy's leg to heal. Even now, slivers of bone still poke through the skin. Michael removes them with tweezers.

There is Emmanuel, eighteen. A little kid when Michael found him living on the street. Real little. Not doing too great.

Real quiet. His father was a hit man—*bungie* in Creole. A criminal for hire. His father supported him but wasn't a father to him. One night some police officers took his father to a field, beat him, and cut his head off. They made Emmanuel watch. That's what will happen if you're like your father, they told him. He was screwed up after that. He's still . . . Michael doesn't know how to say it. The boy has a hard time understanding right from wrong.

There is Nestlie, also eighteen. He lived with his sister after their parents died. They tried to survive on their own but couldn't. Nestlie left his sister to live on the street and make money. He was seven. A lady took him in and used him as a slave. He brought her water and food and cleaned her yard. She gave him more and more to do. She began hitting him. He returned to the street. Some boys he knew told him they lived with a good white guy named Mike. You look terrible, they told him. Come with us.

The tents of a government camp flutter at the bottom of a hill below Camp Benedictine. It is fully occupied and no longer accepting new families, let alone an American with a bunch of street kids. Long, even rows of brand-name tents shimmer in the hazy heat of sunset: Outback, Coleman, Outfitter. It is resplendent in purple-and-white canvas, with little patios and barbecue pits. There is space to spare, several feet at least, between each tent. Paths are paved with crushed white stones. A huge screen shows a movie and stadium lights illuminate the grounds. Music plays. A promised land with outhouses and showers and aromas of food.

Michael sits in a broken plastic chair, head in his hands. His cell phone is out of minutes. There is no money, no money. Kendy closes his eyes and opens them. Closes and opens them again and stares at the government camp below him.

It's real, he says.

Ruth Matringo, an American Airlines stewardess and Airline Ambassadors International volunteer, stops by Camp Benedictine. She met Michael in Port-au-Prince shortly after the earthquake and tries to visit him three times a month. She changes out of her navy blue stewardess uniform into a yellow T-shirt, tan khaki pants, and a baseball cap. She ropes her blond hair into a ponytail and hands Michael a can of Starbucks coffee she brought from Miami.

Hey, stinky, she says to him.

That's right, Michael says. Don't forget it.

She gives him thirty dollars.

That's for you. It's all I have. Don't give it to the kids.

Give me more or I'll break your legs.

Ruth laughs but worries about him. If Michael doesn't take care of himself, how will he take care of the kids? She believes his heart is in the right place but she doesn't see the boys progressing toward any goals. Ruth wonders if that is the real problem. She has never seen Michael discipline the boys. His heart is not in that place. He'll give his left foot for them. He would be lost without them. No matter what, they know they can always come back to him.

You're too much of a giver, she tells him.

Midafternoon. No clouds. Michael forgot his sunscreen, feels his face burning and a headache coming on. He rides a motorcycle to the airport and the offices of UNICEF, his thick red hair pushed back from his forehead by the hot grit-filled breeze peppering his face. He walks the white-graveled grounds of the UNICEF compound, looks at rows and rows of square portable housing, hears the hum of dozens of giant generators. Considers a lot filled with pickup trucks. Peeks inside some of the offices and sees paper plates and plastic forks and knives and cellophane-wrapped trays of food packed in ice and swivel fans turning the still air.

A security guard stops him and asks his name. He tells her about the tents promised to him, but the guard can't find his name on a list of eligible agencies.

You're not here, she tells him.

But I am, he says. This is the seventh time I've been back.

The guard allows him through to the child protection unit of UNICEF.

Do you have an appointment? a receptionist asks him.

No.

You'll have to wait.

He walks outside to the UNICEF PX. He runs his hand over a glass case filled with sunglasses that cost between $90 and $364. He tries to buy a can of the energy drink Battery but the cashier will take only American money. Michael has gourdes, Haitian currency. He stashed the money Ruth gave him in his tent.

That makes a lot of sense, Michael says. I think I'll open a store in New York and accept only gourdes.

He returns to the child protection office. The flustered receptionist scolds him for leaving. The woman he needs to talk to was just here. Where was he? The receptionist walks into another room. She returns followed by a Frenchwoman.

She does not introduce herself to Michael, just starts talking. She tells him UNICEF will do an assessment of his camp in ten days.

You already did an assessment, he says.

Yes, but now we need to assess the assessment.

I don't understand. Listen, all four of our buildings were destroyed. Now we're in shacks. I need to get my kids inside. If we get the tents they'll be inside.

Do you have school?

We won't until we get a tent.

Do you have administrative staff? What plans do you have to clear the land and construct your buildings?

For ten years we had a nice place, Michael says. I still have kids but no place to house them. I need tents.

Make a plan, go to UNICEF, and explain what you need.

Michael takes a deep breath. He understands that UNICEF and other aid agencies have to be careful of scams. He knows that their ability to raise money depends on whether they can show donors that aid isn't being pumped down a rathole. But they've got the wrong guy. He's not scamming. He feels their caution is robbing him of his tents.

You did an assessment and promised me three tents, he says again.

Then we need to assess what we've done.

She holds out her hand but Michael has already turned to leave. The kids won't understand. He tells them something will happen, and when it doesn't they look at him like it's his fault. They don't understand bureaucracy, why it takes so long.

Michael walks across the compound to the office of the Clinton Foundation and asks about his truck.

We're still assessing, a woman tells him. The first run of applicants has been eliminated.

She looks up his name. He remains on the list.

We need transportation, Michael says. We need help.

We haven't been given the go-ahead, the woman tells him. We still have to assess the eligible organizations.

Michael stares at her, speechless, his lined face a road map of fatigue. Cool air stirred by a fan inflates his sweat-damp shirt. He opens the door, hesitates while his eyes adjust to the glare outside.

His frustration spills over at Star 2000 Supermarket, where he stops to charge his cell phone. A security guard tells him to move his motorcycle. Fucking security, Michael shouts at him, I have a right to be here. Fuck your mother, the security guard says. Michael explodes. You call yourself fucking professional! Fucking professional! He rants, jabbing a finger at the security guard, shouting louder and louder and louder, Motherfuckers! But nothing changes. He still has to move his bike. He still won't get his tents. He still won't get his truck. Not today.

There is Bendy, twenty. He had a wonderful mother. She died when he was six. His father sold his two sisters into slavery and kicked Bendy out. He lived with an aunt who used him as a slave. Chained him to a bed. He has scars from the chains around his waist. Beat him. He went hungry. Then he ran away, met Michael.

Bendy was arrested shortly after the earthquake. *Resanblè vòlè*, the police told Michael. He resembles a thief. Michael gave them two tents to release Bendy. Bendy is very protective of Michael and real hard on the other kids. He tells Michael not to tolerate any scams. Just throw them out. Michael explains he can't, they're kids. Bendy disagrees. Little things set him off.

There is Eddie, sixteen. He has epileptic seizures. Scars lace his forehead from falling against rocks, convulsing. He also has a deep scar on his left cheek. Three guys were saying bad things about Michael. Don't say that, Eddie said. Just because he's white, you don't know him. One of them broke a bottle and slashed Eddie's cheek.

There is Dolph, five. He lost his vision when he was two years old to bad voodoo. His parents wanted something big, Michael isn't sure what, and a witch doctor said he would have to take away the boy's sight. The sacrifice was unsuccessful. Dolph's parents didn't get whatever it was they wanted. The father left and the mother abandoned the boy. An orphanage has agreed to take Dolph immediately but Michael needs him in the camp for now. BBC Television has asked to interview Michael in three or four days, and he wants Dolph beside him when they do. A little blind boy. His story will elicit sympathy. With the publicity, Dolph might get sponsors and be set for life. The program might benefit greatly too. Sacrificing a few days until the interview won't kill him.

Dolph's mother must agree to sign him over to the orphanage anyway. She doesn't give a shit, Michael says. He has seen her pin him to the ground with her feet, laughing as he screamed and groped unseeing at the weight on his chest. When Michael started Haitian Street Kids, he was all over the place helping everyone, giving everyone the benefit of the doubt. Not now. Not when he sees people like Dolph's mother.

He was offered a gun once by the police but refused to take it. Walking around or riding a motorcycle with a gun, he knows he'd be asking for it. But nobody fucks with you if you have a gun. Michael has grown harder. He has learned to think like this now.

Two days later three North Carolina missionaries arrive mid-morning with sanitary wipes and a donation of sneakers. At Michael's suggestion, they use Eddie's shack to distribute the shoes. Eddie beams. Bendy scowls. Jealousy thing, Michael knows. But Eddie has the neatest shack. Everything arranged. Clothes and pots and pans suspended against the wall. A sense of organization not seen elsewhere in the camp.

The boys line up outside and enter two at a time. Bendy watches. They remove their sandals and the missionaries wash their feet with the wipes. Evangelists annoy Michael. They always say, You can change your life. He hates that. They assume his life needs changing. They know nothing about him or his boys. Now they will wash the boys' feet and give them socks and shoes. Well, if it gets them some shoes . . .

If I then, your Lord and Teacher, have washed your feet, you also ought to wash one another's feet. For I have given you an example, that you should do as I have done to you, one of the missionaries intones.

The boys watch impassively, argue with the missionaries over shoe sizes. They want the shoes to fit tightly, but the missionaries insist on leaving growing room. The boys leave with the shoes still in their boxes, held at arm's length like rare things. They cover the boxes with T-shirts, protection against the heat and dust, uncertain whether to wear the shoes or keep them like this, always new.

Look what showed up, Michael says. He has an arm around a small boy dressed only in a mud-spattered pair of underpants.

Some people come into the camp and abandon their kids so they have more for themselves, he explains.

He turns the boy around to show huge welts on his back.

Look at the abuse. He's been beaten.

A missionary crouches in front of the boy. The boy backs away. Don't be scared, the missionary says.

The boy speaks to Michael in a barely audible whisper.

What did he say? a missionary asks.

He wants to know what's with all the white people, Michael says.

More and more people come for shoes. The missionaries lose control of the crowd and the shack nearly collapses from the rush of refugees demanding shoes. Walls are ripped open and some of the wood poles supporting the roof collapse. The missionaries stop distributing the shoes and retreat to another part of the camp where they wait for their driver.

When Eddie accuses Bendy of being part of the mob, a shouting match ensues. Other boys get involved and try to restrain them. Bendy stalks off and starts tearing apart his shack. Other members of the camp see what he's doing and begin gathering up whatever he rips away—plastic sheeting, poles, pots and pans.

Bendy, what are you doing? Michael asks him.

Leaving.

Where're you going?

To my family, the street.

Think about what you're doing.

You're not my father, Bendy says.

Bendy—

I have to leave. I am going crazy here. When we had a house we had all these different programs.

Bendy—

No. Not Bendy.

Yesterday I was at—

What about today? What have you done today? Bendy demands.

Think what you're doing.

Bendy leaves, his shack stripped bare of everything but the poles. Then these too are removed by a shirtless old man who looks furtively at Michael.

Michael ignores him, stands on what had been the dry dirt floor of Bendy's home. He bows his head, stares at his shoes. The heat descends in a stultifying embrace. His sweat-drenched shirt and pants weigh him down. He is just so tired. He doesn't know what to do about Bendy or any of them. Tomorrow Bendy will be back, and Michael will be waiting for him. He feels all he does is wait. Wait for tents. Wait for a truck. Wait for something to break his way.

He notices a photograph of himself that belonged to Bendy. He picks it up, crumples it in his palm as his hand folds into a fist.

The next morning, Bendy borrows a cell phone and calls Michael and apologizes. He plans to rebuild his shack on the site of one of Michael's collapsed buildings where he had lived before the earthquake. Michael will check on him, see that he has everything he needs. Then he will force himself to meet with the UNICEF woman again and the people at the Clinton Foundation.

Michael, Michael, Michael.

I'm stressed, a boy tells him.

I'm sorry to hear that, Michael says.

The orphanage that accepted Dolph wants Michael to move in with him. Temporarily. To help Dolph adjust. Michael would have a room, a shower, privacy.

Leave all this for that, he told the boys, standing in the middle of the camp.

He had moved to Haiti because he was tired of living for himself only. Cars. Big-screen TV. A lot of money in the bank. Sitting by himself thinking, What do I do all of this for? So I can watch Showtime? What's the purpose?

No one benefited but him, and he was not really benefiting. He was comfortable, but that was it.

Michael, Michael, Michael.

I didn't get any shoes, another boy says.

What else, what other drama today? Michael asks him.

The problem is that the kids get close to him like a parent and know what buttons to push. They don't understand the bullshit he must endure to get them things. They don't believe him when he tells them he doesn't have money because he always finds a little. He always muddles through somehow. They give him sad puppy dog faces. Like this boy staring at him now, pleading for shoes. He laughs. How can he turn down a puppy?

His laugh turns into a minutes-long cough. Finally he stops, clears his throat, and gropes in his pockets for a cigarette. He thinks of Miami. Maybe he'll spend a night in a Port-au-Prince hotel. Just one night. He pats the boy on the cheek.

We're starting over, he says.

Backyard Battlefields

A year after the gas companies moved in, Dirk DeTurck started taking notes.

> May 2009: Bulldozers started out back building roads and burning trees. House had smoke in it. Like camping indoors. Bought an air purifier.

> May 17, 2009: Started drilling behind house. Noise 24/7. Ears ringing. Still ring. Loud in the house. Roads all torn up. [The gas companies] spread white gooey stuff for dust control . . . Strong diesel smell in the house. Afraid to light a match.

I visited Dirk at his home on the outskirts of Greenbrier, Arkansas, just as a spring heat wave swept through the area. It had rained days before and the trees I passed on the drive over shimmered in the wet heat. Soon, though, the forests gave way to clear-cut areas honeycombed with concrete drill pads. Brown and green tanks rose from the pads; pipes snaked out from pumps.

Uncut forests and bare hills resurged shortly before I arrived at the DeTurcks' stone house, but the wooded acres behind their property struggled to swallow several more pads. The sight was far from threatening to an eye already conditioned to industrial intrusions, but this is a relatively new eyesore in Greenbrier, and Dirk knew better.

He answered the door as if we were in the middle of a conversation started elsewhere. "Hydrogen sulfide hangs in the air like a layer of fog," he said. "It comes off the tanks. Smells like rotten eggs and decaying compost with a little chemical thrown in."

Dirk is a retired mechanic and maintenance man. He studied mechanical engineering in school. He served as a Machinist's Mate in the navy. You name it, he can fix it. He knows how things work.

He and his wife Eva moved to Greenbrier from Elmira, New York, in 2004. Eva had grown up in Mountain View, Arkansas, and Dirk came to love the area after they vacationed there. The land was so primitive, and you couldn't beat the weather.

They chose a home in Greenbrier because it was small and rural and, unlike Mountain View, it had a hospital. Their son had broken forty-three bones after a bad fall from a roof, and subsequent surgery on his aorta left him paralyzed.

The house they found had been built on farmland divided into lots. Dirk and Eva grew a vegetable garden in the backyard. Dirk hunted deer and dried the meat. They were frugal with water and recycled as much as they could. "That's what you're supposed to do," Dirk told me.

In 2004, Dirk had no idea what fracking was. He learned the hard way.

Short for "hydraulic fracturing," fracking is the process by which gas companies access underground deposits of natural

gas, called shales. Millions of gallons of "fracking fluid"—
that's water and sand mixed with hundreds of chemicals—are
pumped deep into the earth's crust, breaking up rock and
freeing natural gas reserves.

Natural gas is being marketed as a clean, green alternative
to foreign oil dependency; this year, the International Energy
Agency found that energy-production-related carbon dioxide
emissions in the U.S. fell by 450 tons, the result of an increase
in the use of natural gas instead of coal. But since the incep-
tion of widespread fracking in 1997, horror stories have slowly
entered the national conscience: illnesses possibly tied to contaminated wells, citizens who can light their tap water on fire,
pet and livestock deaths, exploding houses.

"The industry says [fracking fluid] goes down and comes
back up through pipes and is fine," says Daniel Botkin, an ecol-
ogist and professor emeritus at the University of California,
Santa Barbara. "In fact, stuff comes out and contaminates surface water and soil. If they wanted to do this in any reliable
way, they would pick a few places and frack as an experiment
and study the outcomes. That's not what's happening. There's
so much money to be made, fracking is done on a very large
scale. It could affect a lot of people."

Much of northern Arkansas, including Greenbrier, sits atop
the Fayetteville Shale, one of the largest natural gas reserves
in the country. Oil and gas companies began developing the
area in late 2004; today, approximately four thousand gas wells
plumb the depths of the shale. The Sam M. Walton College of
Business at the University of Arkansas estimates that the first
five years of Fayetteville Shale exploration generated 11,000
jobs and $18 billion in revenue.

September 2009: Rash started on waist, armpits.
Spread to knees. I didn't know what started it.
Face and neck tingle like something crawling on it.
Tongue bleeding for no reason.

When construction equipment started rumbling by in 2008, Dirk and Eva thought someone was damming Mill Creek for water supply to a nearby town. Then they noticed the trucks inching down Blackjack Road—ten to twelve eighteen-wheelers a day.

"Are they bulldozing to build houses?" Dirk asked a neighbor.

"No," the man said. "They're drilling gas wells."

At night, the gas pads blazed as if someone had switched on stadium lights. The drilling sent vibrations through the house and the noise filled every room, making it impossible to talk. Black smoke ringed the tops of trees. The air carried sharp, stinging odors. Magnolias and blue spruce began dying; deer, turkeys, raccoons, and opossums disappeared. Dirk found the bodies of tumorous squirrels whose tails had fallen off.

For the next year, Dirk and Eva kept their doors and windows closed. They no longer sat on their deck. Their four grandchildren were not allowed to play outside the house for more than two hours; if they were out longer, they got headaches. Despite the precaution, one of the boys developed a rash. The doctor chalked it up to an allergy, prescribed a steroid cream.

Eva, meanwhile, was unable to sleep. She felt jittery, jacked up. Then Dirk noticed his own rashes. His nose began bleeding. His tongue began bleeding.

January 1, 2011: Tap water turned light brown. Cleared up same day. Started getting pink rings in toilet bowls. What is in water?

Whatever was in the water, the DeTurcks decided to quit drinking it. Eva also started taking motion sickness pills to cope with the earthquakes, which had been rattling the area since 2009. In December 2010, civic leaders scheduled a community meeting in which geologists explained how earthquakes worked, but failed to account for the severe uptick in tremors. The large congregation of concerned citizens turned sour, and the meeting was broken up by sheriffs.

At the request of the Arkansas Oil and Gas Commission, Haydar Al-Shukri, the chair of the Department of Applied Science at the University of Arkansas, Little Rock, had been monitoring an injection well in the Greenbrier area. Reinjection into the ground is one of several methods by which gas companies dispose of the fluid that makes its way back up to the surface after fracking. Al-Shukri's equipment was able to detect seismic activity within a twenty-five-mile radius that included three other injection wells. In 2009, he found a strong correlation between the earthquakes and two of the wells.

"They were very close to the fault," Al-Shukri said. "Injection wells close to the fault can cause the fault to slip." In February 2011, the Greenbrier area experienced a quake that registered 4.7 on the Richter scale—the state's worst in thirty-five years. A month later, when a moratorium was placed on the injection wells, the earthquakes all but stopped. In the six months prior to the shutdown, over 1,200 earthquakes had been recorded.

Then in March, when two injection wells were shut down,

the earthquakes all but stopped. However, gas drilling and fracking continued, though now the used fracking fluid had to be transported to injection wells outside the area.

About the same time the earthquakes began to subside, Dirk noticed numbers on the tanks of the trucks he saw coming and going from the drill sites. He knew from work experience that the numbers were assigned by the United Nations Committee of Experts on the Transport of Dangerous Goods, and are meant to alert emergency crews to activate hazard-specific procedures in case of a wreck or spill. Dirk recorded all of the numbers he saw, along with notes like "Saw driving through a school zone."

Under an exemption pushed through Congress in 2005, the contents of fracking fluid are considered proprietary; in other words, oil and gas companies are under no obligation to disclose which chemicals they use, so they don't. Independent efforts like Dirk's, however, suggest fracking fluid often contains antifreeze, detergents, known human carcinogens, and neurotoxins.

Memphis lawyer Tim Holton wants courts to require independent monitoring of water supplies and public health in areas near fracking activities. He is representing a number of Arkansas families who claim fracking has damaged their health.

Horton tells me of a family he represents—two children who live with their grandparents. In August 2011, three natural gas wells were placed within 250 feet of their home. Their suit alleges that, during the fracking process, large amounts of xylene, methylene chloride, and benzene were released and contaminated the air inside the home to toxic levels. Several fracking procedures can cause volatile organic compounds, or VOCs, to become airborne.

Long-term xylene exposure can cause harm to the nervous system, liver, and kidneys. Prolonged exposure to methylene chloride can cause neurological damage. Benzene is a carcinogen.

"I was amazed by the extent of emissions wafting over the home. It looked like a refinery in Texas but it was one frack site," Holton says. "The health effects of this are in their infancy in Arkansas. The effect won't be seen for several years. You sit around breathing it in and you won't know right away what it's doing. You'll have no idea. Then you turn forty-five and you can't draw a breath."

The sign right outside of Guy, Arkansas, reads: *Welcome to Guy. A Small Town with a Big Heart.* It's about a ten-minute drive from Dirk's house. I spoke to the mayor there, Johnny Wilson.

Mayor Wilson tells me the gas companies employ lots of people in Guy. Folks have been moving in from Louisiana, Oklahoma, Texas. Going on six years now. The population shot up to 708 when a few years back it was just 203. A fracking company employs Wilson's own son.

"They're just jealous," he says of citizens who criticize the gas companies. He chuckles. "They don't have mineral rights to sell. The naysayers don't get checks and that makes them mad."

Jackie McPherson, the mayor of Heber Springs, Arkansas, is equally enthusiastic about the industry. He tells me natural gas saved his town from the recession. Sure, it staggered during the hardest times, but people were still going to jobs or getting royalty checks. They bought homes and new cars. Some had never bought new cars before. Since the drilling started, people have moved in from other states. Hotels filled with oil prospectors. Despite the recession, the tax base of Heber Springs is growing.

Mayor McPherson has lived in Heber Springs since 1964. He's the president of the local waterskiing club. He owns two boats. No one, he says, wants to protect the environment like he does.

I ask Mayor Wilson for the names of people he knows who got work through the gas companies. I call each one but they all refuse to talk to me when I identify myself as a reporter, save for one man. The man says he would still be "kicking the can down the road" if the gas companies hadn't given him a job. Before he speaks further or agrees to let me use his name, he says he needs to ask his work supervisor for permission. He says he'll get right back to me. He never does.

Tracy Wilson and her husband Keith, an Iraq War veteran, live in a white house with a broad front porch. Two llamas stand fenced-in beyond their gravel drive. Keith is hosing out animal pens as I drive up, his shorts and shirt soaked. Tracy comes out of the house on crutches, blond hair playing off her shoulders.

Keith is a police officer. Tracy takes in exotic species people once owned as pets but can no longer manage. Llamas, bobcat, lynx, and wild deer are among the wildlife in their care. They speak to me on the condition that I not mention where they live, for fear someone might try to steal their animals.

The Wilsons grew up near Little Rock, but decided to leave the city for the country when Tracy started her wildlife sanctuary. The property they chose offered plenty of space; none of their neighbors lived on fewer than ten acres. Many of the families around them raised beef and dairy cows. After she and Keith moved in, Tracy planted a thousand pines to create even more privacy.

In 2005, the Wilsons heard rumors that oil companies would soon be drilling for gas in the Fayetteville Shale. They began receiving letters from those same companies, offering to buy their mineral rights for one hundred dollars an acre. The amount increased with each letter. Two hundred, two hundred and fifty. Tracy tossed them. Neither she nor Keith was interested. Tracy bought more pines, thinking the trees would create a buffer between their home and the wells.

The pines, however, were not enough to prevent landmen from stopping by the house. Petroleum landmen perform various services for oil and gas exploration companies. According to the American Association of Professional Landmen's website, these services include negotiating for the acquisition and divestiture of mineral rights.

The men who came by the Wilsons' house knew their business. Hair slicked back, fresh pressed shirts. They told Tracy her mineral rights could be worth hundreds of thousands of dollars. They told her she would pay cash for new Cadillacs. She asked the landmen to show her something in writing, but they never did. Instead, they threatened to have the property condemned if Tracy and Keith didn't sell their mineral rights voluntarily.

Tracy thought they were bluffing and spoke to an attorney. The attorney told her that a gas company could appeal to the Arkansas Oil and Gas Commission. State laws can force a homeowner to turn over his mineral rights if everyone else in his sector has leased his. "Forced pooling" compels holdout landowners to join gas-leasing agreements with their neighbors. In Arkansas, drillers can extract minerals from an entire pool if leases have been negotiated for a certain percentage of the land.

The attorney advised the Wilsons to work out a lease wherein they sold their mineral rights for $450 an acre. They kept their property rights, however, so the gas companies could not drill within 500 feet of their property. It was flimsy protection; if the gas company changed its mind and decided to drill on their property, it could just take them to court. The Wilsons didn't have the money to fight them.

In 2008, helicopters dropped fiber-optic cables and depth charges for seismic tests, Tracy recalls. A gas well went in within 1,800 feet of the Wilsons' house. When the drilling started, the Wilsons' house shook as if a train were running through it. Twenty-four hours, seven days a week.

In 2009, Tracy started getting dizzy. Her head ached. She broke out in rashes. She smelled something like plastic burning. At night, she would shine a flashlight and see particulates in the air. *I'm breathing that stuff in*, she thought.

That was the year Keith returned from his second deployment in Iraq. When he saw the gas wells near his house, he was reminded of the oil plants in Iraq, the noise of drill rigs. Soldiers, he told Tracy, were coming back with respiratory problems from inhaling smoke coming off the oil wells and the trash pits on U.S. bases, where everything from discarded human body parts to plastics were burned. He smelled that same stench again, only this time in his backyard.

Keith didn't want to think about Iraq, but the tankers and water trucks reminded him of the vehicles he'd seen in Iraq's oil fields. In Iraq, if an eighteen-wheeler pulled up on him, it either backed off or got blown away.

Tracy had headaches for the entire month of August 2010. Skin lesions and blisters broke out on her back. Her lymph nodes swelled to golf ball size, she says. Her doctor gave her antibiotics and topical creams, but nothing worked. Keith developed nosebleeds; he'd never had them before. His nose would start running and there would be blood.

A month before the big quake, Tracy blacked out and fell down the stairs. She tore a tendon and chipped a bone in her left ankle. The bone refused to heal. Her doctor didn't know why.

I break off our conversation for a moment and call Adam Law, a clinical assistant professor at Weill Cornell Medical College and practicing endocrinologist in New York. He is calling on gas companies to stop the use of hydraulic fracturing until its effects on people and the environment have been thoroughly studied. I tell him about the symptoms the Wilsons and DeTurcks experienced.

"As doctors, we're not really trained in environmental health," he says. "There's very little training with occupational exposure. When you see stuff like this for the first time, it's a little uncomfortable. You don't know who to send the patient to or what to prescribe. It's difficult to know what they've been exposed to. You can tell people how to reduce exposure—don't bathe or drink the water—but it's hard to say don't breathe."

Tracy and Keith had planned to retire on their land and never move again. In 2009, they spent $70,000 on improvements to the fourteen-year-old house; they upgraded the sunroom, replaced the roof, put in new central air, painted inside and out. They had the house appraised when they finished in 2011. It was valued at $70,000 less than it had been in 2009. Back then, there wasn't as much traffic. There weren't gas wells nearby.

When the big quake struck, the Wilsons' dogs, roosters, and donkeys began barking and crowing and braying all at once. The ground shifted. A kind of growl passed through the house. The noise was like thunder, Keith says, but it lasted longer. They bought earthquake insurance for $800 a year—more than any royalty payment they have received from the gas company.

From the Wilsons' house, I drive west to Hartford, Arkansas, to meet Jack and Mary White. They live on a stretch of road flanked by tall grass and scrub brush. Cows poke their heads through warped fences and the cloudless sky wavers from an oppressive heat.

Jack is eighty-two years old. Mary uses a cane to walk. Jack helps her, crouching forward a little bit, a hand on her elbow. After lunch, Jack drives me to a graveyard called Sugar Loaf Cemetery. A creek runs not far from it. Water brought people here to Hartford, Jack says. Since the 1800s, the people have depended on water for their farms, crops, and cattle.

In 2005, when a landman knocked on Jack's door, he knew what was coming. Jack had been an oilman himself. After he was honorably discharged from the Air Force during the Korean War, his older brother got him a job working the oil fields in West Texas. He started as a roughneck, then became an oil well servicer, a driller, and, later, a superintendent. He met Mary in Kermit right after she finished high school. A mutual friend said, "Oh, there's Mary," and introduced them. Jack doesn't know how these things work out, but they do.

Jack worked oil in Egypt and Iran in the early sixties. He and Mary returned to the States in 1966 so their son could attend high school here. When they moved to Hartford, they planned to retire and produce organic food for their livelihood and sustenance. Jack wanted to put in hoop houses beside their house. In a hoop house, vegetables don't know it's winter, he says. You don't have insect problems. The vegetables taste sweeter, crisper. Hoop houses need a lot of water, so Jack drilled a well.

"I'm a farm boy at heart," he tells me. "Some of my people have lived in Arkansas and Oklahoma forever. There's no such thing as worn-out soil. There is neglect and abuse."

In 2006, the gas company drilled a well to extract water for fracking, Jack says. Their well was deeper than his, and drew his water away. His water pump came up dry. Nowadays it occasionally kicks in, but doesn't pull enough water for hoop houses. "I have to pick and choose what lives and what dies," he says.

"When they drill a gas well," Jack continues, "they blow all the liquid and dust out of the hole. Sounds like a scream rushing out of the ground." The fracking noise started as a roar before it rose to the pitch of a siren. Days, weeks. Jack quit counting after a while. Twelve diesel compressors added to the racket. Jack and Mary got desperate for sleep and rented motel rooms. They came back to the house as much as they could, so that it wouldn't appear abandoned, but people knew they were gone. Someone raided their shed and stole Jack's tools.

One day, when the gas company was blowing out a well, Jack was on a neighbor's property helping him clear brush. When he got back to his house, he found Mary lying prostrate on the floor. She'd inhaled too much methane, he says. A doctor told Jack that ten minutes later might have been too late.

Jack says Mary has never been the same. He says oilmen used to have more respect, but he understands there's a lot of money to be made. He's angry at the State of Arkansas for failing to regulate, failing to protect. He wonders if he'll have enough water to fend off a summer of record heat. He wonders how many more of his neighbors will clear out before it's over. After traveling to over sixty foreign countries, he still thinks Hartford is the best place on earth.

"We're not gonna go anyplace else," he says. "At our age, it's just too late."

> May 2012: Last two days, ears popping. Metal taste in mouth.

These days, the DeTurcks sit in their living room and peer out closed windows at their empty wood deck. They've noticed birds and squirrels returning, but still don't see any turkeys or more than a few deer. Their health improved somewhat after they installed an air purifier designed to remove VOCs, but Eva still developed little bumps on her chin. When the wind blows away from the house, Dirk notices his rashes begin to clear.

He and Eva have put the house up for sale. An Arizona couple looked at the house and offered to buy it. They had two boys, ten and twelve. "Do you know about the gas drilling here?" Dirk asked them. They said no. Dirk refused to sell. How could he sleep at night believing that those two boys were being poisoned?

Tracy Wilson still has trouble with her ankle. As of June 2012, she's been reliant on crutches for eighteen months. She says the gas companies come and go without contacting residents. She wakes up and *oopsy*, there's a new crane or rig.

One night in May, Tracy woke up feeling something wet on her back. Another open abscess. Clear fluid draining from it. Some of her cats have half-dollar-size blisters that look like burns. "We got ourselves chemical hazard suits and emergency kits, complete with gas masks, to have on hand in case of a chemical spill or worse," she writes in an email. "Who lives with emergency chemical hazard kits hanging on their coatrack in their home?"

Keith dreams of Iraq. In one dream, he walks across a battle-field picking up weapons amid the eerie orange glow of burning wells. For a long time, he didn't understand why he dreamed that dream night after night. Then he understood.

In Iraq, Keith passed an oil well on his left every time he went on patrol. When he returned to base, he would pass another well on his right. Now, when he leaves the house for work, he sees a gas well to his left. Returning home, he notices another well on his right.

Every day he sees Iraq.

When I leave the Wilsons' house, I make a wrong turn and get lost on a gravel road. I stop at a convenience store and ask for directions to Highway 65.

The man behind the counter tells me to go west. He says I'll see a lot of tanker trucks that haul water and chemicals to gas pads. Then a lot of white pickups, some with gas company names on the side, but not all. And then lots of dump trucks, the ones that run dirt and gravel to the pads.

Once you're on 65, he tells me, it'll take a while to get past the drilling. After that, the drive up is beautiful, especially with the trees this time of year. You won't see quite as many gas pads with the trees all leafed-out. You won't know they're there.

Nothing Went to Waste:
Considering the Life of Ben Kennedy

Sometime in the late 1970s, early 1980s, a man named Ben Kennedy wandered into the Montana Nature Conservancy near downtown Helena. He stopped by the open office door of its director at the time, Bob Kiesling.

Hi, Ben said. What is it you people do?

Who is this old fart asking questions? Bob remembered thinking. Then he recognized Ben as the elderly guy he had seen walking around town for years with a big plastic bag, collecting cans.

Ben sat down. Bob did all the talking and Ben listened. In fact, he paid rapt attention. He didn't ask questions, just said, That's good, or I like that, or That makes sense. He showed an understanding of environmental issues; the impact of building roads in national forests, pollution, saving wildlife habitat. On his way out, Ben thrust a hand into a pants pocket and pulled out four crumpled $100 bills. You know, I appreciate what you're doing and want to make a contribution to the effort, he said.

No, Ben, Bob said, waving him off. Spend this on a meal, for God's sake. Keep it. Don't worry about us.

Ben, however, insisted. In the coming months, he would drop by without notice and give Bob donations of $200 or $300.

Brian Kahn, the host of the Montana Public Radio program *Home Ground Radio*, encountered Ben about ten years after Bob first met him. Brian had replaced Bob as director of the conservancy. Brian kept his office door open too, and one day Ben asked to come in. Brian answered his questions about the conservancy just as Bob had. He thought Ben was shy, self-effacing, and soft-spoken. He was also inquisitive and sharp, and never took his eyes off Brian. His questions were not broad or detailed; he seemed less interested in the program than in what Brian revealed about himself. After two or three questions, Brian had the impression that Ben had enough information to decide whether he was on the level.

Later, when Brian learned that Ben knew Bob and had been giving money to the conservancy for years, he concluded that Ben had been sizing him up as Bob's replacement.

Ben approved. He gave Brian $200.

People who knew Ben Kennedy told me he didn't talk much. If he liked someone, he would often drop by unannounced, content to sit silently in their company. In this way he got to know a number of people around Helena, people like Bob and Brian. They became good acquaintances, if not friends.

Ben was born in 1922 in Belt, Montana, and died in 2009 just short of his eighty-seventh birthday. His long gray hair sprouted from his head and his windblown beard grew thick and wild about his face. His smile exposed a mouthful of ruined teeth and many that just weren't there. Most people who didn't know him assumed he was homeless.

Much to their surprise, the old man left a mark on his adopted city of Helena by squirreling away money from his monthly Social Security stipend and transforming it into the handfuls of cash he produced from his pockets and gave to a few local environmental entities he thought mattered.

He stood about five feet seven and liked a beer or a cup of tea with his soup more than he liked to bathe. He wore baggy long-sleeved shirts and polyester pants and shoes with Velcro straps that he bought at Goodwill. He didn't bother with socks. He owned an old gray Subaru hatchback but walked everywhere or rode a bike. He scavenged newspapers and aluminum cans for recycling because he believed nothing should go to waste. He had a bank account but never kept more than $3,000 in it before he started giving his money away. He didn't make pledges or monthly dona-tions; he gave when he had accumulated some money—$100, $200, $400. When he died, he left little of it behind.

A short notice about his death in the *New York Times* didn't tell me much, just enough to make me want to put this guy in a box, tidy him up with neat explanations about his philan-thropy, and forget about him. But I couldn't. I had been a social worker before I became a journalist and had known many poor people who, after they died, left surprising amounts of money to charitable organizations that had helped them. I had never, however, known someone like Ben Kennedy, who gave money to agencies that had never offered him assistance of any kind, and who chose to live a virtually monastic life.

Why? A reporting assignment in Montana gave me the opportunity to find out. Perhaps, I thought, he was a hail-fel-low-well-met type who chose to hand out money rather than have a good steak once in a while. Possibly he went all Zen at some point and had an epiphany about material things, the self. Maybe he was just odd, if not crazy.

None of these explanations satisfied me. In his quiet, unassuming way, despite what in a social context might be dismissed as eccentric behavior, Ben at the very least was a man who invited stereotype only to defy expectations. He went at life mostly from the outside looking in. He was the original no-impact man, somebody who with his meager dollars and with his day-to-day, minute-to-minute existence chose not to bruise the planet any more than he had to. He didn't leave much of a legacy, but in a way that was his legacy.

Nothing went to waste.

A zippered sleeping bag lay on the floor in the one-bedroom apartment Ben rented in the subsidized M. E. Anderson Apartments. A green plastic lawn chair took up a corner of the living room. Gray wall-to-wall carpeting covered the floor, and neighbors had complained about the smell from the cans he collected and stored in bags until he took them to a recycling center. His refrigerator was empty.

Ben Kennedy is a slight man, a reporter for the *Billings Gazette* wrote in a January 2003 article about Meals on Wheels. He wears his hair and beard long. Long gone gray, he's intent on ensuring that two fellow residents in his apartment complex get their lunch on time.

He knows what it's like to live on $10 worth of food stamps a month. In fact, he does. That's why he relies on Meals on Wheels to bring him a cooked meal five days a week. It's the only full, hot meal he and a few others living in the M. E. Anderson Apartments eat each day.

He guided Meals on Wheels workers to the correct apartment doors one day last week.

"The meal is a big help," Kennedy said modestly while accepting his lunch of spaghetti, garlic bread, beans, and fruit cocktail.

The Windbag Saloon & Grill, a restaurant in Helena's downtown outdoor mall, became a stopping-off point for Ben. He would hang out for an hour or so, say hello to acquaintances, but little more. He stood at one end of the bar or the other and would have a short glass of beer with some soup. He never entered the restaurant. When he finished his beer, he would dump what foam remained in his glass into his soup bowl and scrape the bowl clean. He refused offers of a napkin and a coaster. He thought they were a waste of paper.

You didn't small-talk Ben, Jerry Foley, a retired state employee and a regular at the Windbag, told me. Hi, how you doing, Ben? He'd throw it right back. Oh, I'm doing okay, and that was that.

Ben was about the same age as Jerry's father and always asked about him. He's fine, Jerry would say. How're you? In this way they began talking, and on occasion Ben would reveal small amounts of information about himself. One afternoon he told Jerry he had been thrown out of college when he hit on a male student and administrators found out he was gay. He had wanted to be a teacher. He felt he'd gotten screwed. But then his mood lightened and Ben joked that gay people should get an award as the solution to overpopulation. He laughed a kind of tee-hee laugh. Not loud. A rural laugh. An old-timer's laugh. He said, I don't know how so-called Christians can say such-and-such. He shook his head and laughed that laugh again.

One late evening at the Windbag, as Jerry and Ben talked, Jerry began scribbling notes on a bar napkin. Ben had been telling him about his service in World War II. *83rd Ohio Div France 1 wk after Normandy,* Jerry wrote. To this day he doesn't know why he took notes or why he kept the napkin. He was about to throw it away when I drove into Helena and began asking questions about Ben. Jerry gave me the napkin, suggesting that if it was not divine intervention that he had kept it so long, it was Ben guiding him from the grave.

The army's 83rd Infantry Division, nicknamed the Ohio Division, arrived in England on April 16, 1944. After training in Wales, the division landed at Omaha Beach on June 18 and faced strong opposition as it moved inland. Months later it fought in the Battle of the Bulge and then continued to advance toward Germany. It found more than a thousand emaciated inmates in Langenstein, a subunit of the Buchenwald concentration camp. Many of the prisoners were too weak to survive after their liberation, and dozens of men, women, and children died each day. Ben never said he was at the Battle of the Bulge or Langenstein; he told Jerry only that he'd arrived in Normandy about a week after the D-day invasion.

Ben rarely talked about the war, his niece Judith Gedrose said. Her mother, Ben's sister, said he had changed after the war but never explained how, despite Judith's questions. When she tried to show him photographs of France, he refused to look at them.

Her mother didn't like Ben, Judith said. Judith tried to engineer outings with brother and sister but neither was interested. She never learned what had caused the rift. Ben was the sixth of nine children. Despite the death of his parents when he was still a boy, he and his eight siblings lived well growing up. They had a housekeeper. Their father had provided them with trust funds, and they made it through the Depression. As a young man, Ben wore pressed shirts and was clean-shaven. Except for a brother who stayed in Belt to operate a hardware store, the rest of the family left town.

Sitting in her room in a Butte nursing home, his sister Izzy, eighty-seven, told me Ben was different. Not as a child, but when he got older. I asked if she was referring to his appearance or the fact that he was gay. She would not say. We grew up and went our separate ways, Izzy told me.

Ben and Judith would take walks together in Helena. He liked to say, Other people can believe what they believe—that's okay. But some things, he thought, were not okay. He spoke to Judith about being gay. He felt he had been discriminated against, and he wanted to help other people who had been too. Sometimes he would get agitated. He argued with tenants and management in his apartment building about the use of air-conditioning in the dining area. He thought it was wasteful.

Brian Kahn's wife, Montana landscape painter Sandra Dal Poggetto, had on occasion driven Ben home to his apartment. It was a place for low-income people, she said. His room was on the south side, and he would complain about it being very hot in the summer. The Kahns sometimes invited Ben to dinner. He didn't speak unless spoken to. One time, he sat on their couch entranced by the flute-playing of James Galway on the CD player.

Bob Kiesling remembers that Ben mentioned some of the people in his building but said nothing that suggested lasting friendships. I don't have a telephone but I can run up to Richard's room, Ben would tell him. He drinks too much but he'll let me use his phone.

A few years before he died, Ben met a woman at a local senior center not far from his apartment. He bought her a $400 set of tires for her car. She would take him to Real Food Market & Deli, an organic supermarket, where he'd buy items on his debit card. One day he turned the card over to her and asked her to go to the store for him. Overdraft notices started coming in. Ben went to Bob for help, and Bob took him to the bank. A bank representative was sympathetic and forgave all the fees and interest charges. He got into that mess because he wanted companionship, Bob said. I wasn't surprised. I was surprised that his need for companionship hadn't overwhelmed him more often.

Brian Kahn disagreed. On the contrary, he thought Ben had created a self-contained world in which he was very comfortable alone. It may have been that he made a virtue out of necessity, Brian observed.

One afternoon toward the end of his life when Ben stopped by the Nature Conservancy, he appeared weak and shaky, Susan Benedict, the director of administration, told me. She drove him to the emergency room. He was nervous in the hospital, and she put a hand on his leg to reassure him. She thought the doctors had been rude and impatient with him. Maybe they'd seen Ben before and were tired of him. They said he might just have the flu. Afterward she took him home. The sleeping bag on the floor. The empty refrigerator. She said nothing. He didn't like it if anyone commented on how he lived.

He knew what his priorities were, she said. Why have things, he told her, when that money could be given to good causes like the Nature Conservancy? Giving was a way for him to get attention from people he admired. He wanted to hang with people who made it happen, make contact.

Ben never explained why he was so devoted to environmental organizations. People who knew he was gay were intrigued that a man of his generation was comfortable being out of the closet, that he felt somewhat political about gay rights and yet he spent what little money he had on eco causes.

We live on the planet, Ben once told Brian Khan. We have to take care of it. It makes sense.

In the mid-1990s Ben had an operation for an enlarged prostate and one of his testicles was removed. He sank into a deep depression. He wanted to end his life. He told Jerry Foley, I hope I die. A retired physician and friend of Bob Kiesling visited Ben and told him it was normal for prostate patients to get depressed. Don't check out. Hang in there. Six months later, he was chipper again.

Yet his depression on occasion would return. Brian Kahn rarely spoke to Ben by phone, but he remembered one time in particular when he had. Ben was having an anxiety attack. He was worried that he was losing his mental acuity.

Shortly after Ben recovered from his prostate operation, in about 1997, he told Bob, I'd like to get to Belt and live out my days there and buy a house. But he had no savings with which to make a down payment and gave up on the idea about as fast as he had thought of it. Belt lies about thirteen miles north of Great Falls. A narrow road twists down through a tree-lined gorge before it flattens out into what had been a paved main street but is now mostly dirt and broken asphalt. The street winds past two-story nineteenth-century brick storefronts: Harvest Moon Saloon; Farmers & Miners State Bank, now the city hall; and the vacant Belt Hardware Company.

Ben's older brother Earl had taken over management of the hardware store for his mother at age eighteen, following the death of his father. The business closed during World War II and reopened in 1946. In 1960 it closed for the final time, and the building was sold to the Belt Valley Bank. Ben was named after his father, who was born in Illinois in 1879. Ben senior moved to Montana around 1900 and to Belt in 1913. Three years later he purchased the hardware store. Residents recalled how horse-drawn wagons were stored on the top floor, hoisted up by a rope elevator. Earl, who died in southern Nevada in 2005, was remembered as a quiet man. Gerald Maberry, a Belt resident since 1950, saw Ben when he came up from Helena with Bob Kiesling to look into the cost of a house. He resembled a hobo who had just jumped off a freight train, Gerald said. Ben had a camera, and wandered around snapping pictures. He told Gerald he had not been back to Belt in years.

When a house in Belt was no longer an option, Ben decided to give Great Falls a try. He was growing increasingly unhappy in his apartment and didn't want to remain in Helena. His neighbors complained about him because his carpet had absorbed the odors from all the cans he had collected, and the stink could be smelled in the hall. After World War II, Ben had lived in Great Falls and worked as a receptionist at the *Great Falls Tribune*. Bob Kiesling checked out assisted-care places and found several that would accept Ben, but he refused. He liked his independence and doing as he pleased, which included attending exhibitions at the Turman Gallery in Helena (now the Turman-Larison Contemporary). Ben told gallery owner Doug Turman that he had been to art shows in Washington and Boston when he returned from France. Doug would urge him to eat. Now look, Ben, try this, and he would point to a plate of hors d'oeuvres. Ben would stay about ten minutes, have a cup of coffee, maybe two. He never took food away with him.

Ben always bought lottery tickets. He told Doug that if he won, he would give the money to the Nature Conservancy. He asked Doug to claim the winning ticket for him should that day ever come. He did not want the publicity. He said he wasn't interested in having a park bench named after him.

A few months before he died, Ben called Bob Kiesling and said he felt weak. Can you check on me? he asked. Bob went over to Ben's apartment and took him some soup. Eat the soup, Ben, he told him. Ben's eyes rolled back in his head and he fell over backward, before Bob could catch him. His head hit the floor and made a godawful sound and he began twitching. Bob called 911. He knew Ben didn't want extraordinary measures taken to save him. He had drafted a living will with Bob's help but had never authorized it.

I don't want to be here, Ben told Bob at the hospital. He returned to his apartment and all but stopped eating. It wasn't a complete fast leading to death, Bob told me, but over a period of several months it did him in. He was ready.

Brian Khan visited Ben in his apartment after he was released from the hospital. Ben was frail and had lost so much weight he was almost skeletal. He seemed confused, anxious. He would stand up and then lie back down on his sleeping bag. He was worried. He wondered whether the human race would outlive all the problems facing it and the planet. He was pessimistic about the outcome.

As his health declined, Ben gave Bob Kiesling a key to his apartment so Bob could look in on him. On the morning of December 2, 2009, Ben didn't answer his knock and Bob let himself in. He found Ben on his right side, half curled on his sleeping bag. Bob assumed he was asleep, but when he didn't stir, he checked his pulse.

In the days following Ben's death, Bob cleared out his apartment. The other tenants sorted through the few things Ben owned—his sleeping bag, kitchen utensils, clothes—and took what they wanted.

Nothing went to waste.

On December 16, 2009, Ben's acquaintances gathered at the Windbag to remember him. Jerry Foley was surprised by how packed the place was. He hadn't known that Ben made cash donations to environmental organizations.

Jerry told me that he misses Ben. He recycles more. He tries not to make snap judgments based on the way people look. He has adopted one of Ben's expressions: It is what it is. Others who attended Ben's memorial were still sorting out what Ben meant to them. Occasionally I think about him, Susan Benedict of the conservancy told me. I appreciated Ben, but he was not someone I wanted to spend a lot of time with. I didn't understand his extreme lifestyle. He was not rooted in things. I try to live with less, but I'm caught up in consumerism like anyone else. It is what it is.

I left Helena a short time after I spoke to Susan. Ben remained a mystery to me. His life had very little to do with the way most of us would want to live. By setting aside his self-interest for the sake of others, Ben upended an ethos that has so far dominated the twenty-first century the same way it consumed the twentieth. How many of us, after all, really sort out what we think is important and focus our energy as much as possible on that? Ben provided no easy answers.

Bob Kiesling made arrangements for Ben's body to be cremated. He still has the box of ashes in his office in a cardboard tub from the crematorium. One day he will scatter the ashes over a nice spot in Belt. He will shake them into the ground at the base of a tree or on some flowers in need and offer to the earth Ben Kennedy's final donation.

What Happens After Sixteen Years in Prison?

They still talk about it here in Hillsboro.

How the Scott sisters, Jamie and Gladys, were arrested for organizing an armed robbery they say they had no part in. How Jamie, twenty-one, and Gladys, just nineteen, neither one of whom had a police record or even a speeding ticket, were each given two consecutive life sentences for the crime, far more time than the boys who were either their accomplices or who falsely claimed to be. How no one can even say how much money was stolen, if any. Some accounts put the figure at eleven dollars.

After serving sixteen years, the sisters were released in the first few days of 2011. Governor Haley Barbour suspended their sentences on the condition that Gladys donate a kidney to Jamie, whose own kidneys had begun to fail a year earlier. She has not done so yet.

The Scott sisters live in Pensacola now. They moved there to be with their mother, Evelyn Rasco. Miss Evelyn herself lies critically ill in a local hospital, her left leg amputated as a result of her own battle with diabetes.

Sixteen years I fought, she mumbles in her sleep. I'm tired.

But in Hillsboro, not that much has changed since Jamie and Gladys were sent to prison. The town is little more than a dot on the map seven miles outside Forest, Mississippi, a slightly bigger dot just off Interstate 20. Turn off the interstate onto Highway 35, following the road through the woods where, on starless nights, the darkness seems as deep and still as the ocean, and after a few miles you'll drive past a few motels and a Kentucky Fried chicken before you reach the mini-mart where Jamie's car broke down the night the crime took place. The girls caught a ride there with two boys who later said the sisters had led them into an ambush.

The Scott sisters' father, James Rasco, was born and raised in Hillsboro. The family goes way back. Black children here are taught to stay out of trouble. Keep your head down and just get on with your life. At night, enjoy yourself, but stay in the house. And when you're out, hope no police get behind you. Looked like you swerved, they'll say. What're you all dressed up for? Getting into something? You know so-and-so? Don't let the police pin nothing on you, people here say. You'll end up like Jamie and Gladys.

Jamie and Gladys awaken before dawn in Pensacola. Miles apart from each other, each in her own home, hearing nothing but the sound of their own breathing. In prison, they were surrounded by hundreds of other women. Hundreds of women watching one another, talking all at once, almost touching. Someone would be screaming over the intercom and someone else would be blasting the TV and at the same time there'd be showers hissing and the microwave beeping and a dozen toilets flushing. Noise bouncing off concrete. There were women who raped other women. There were fights. Once a girl threw boiling water on another girl she'd been arguing with; the skin peeled off the second girl's face like mud sliding downhill.

They'd gotten into it over the TV. The girl who'd thrown the water had wanted to watch a soap. She boiled the water in the microwave good and hot.

In Pensacola, Jamie and Gladys get up, make their beds. The routine was drilled into them in prison: up at five, make your bed, or get written up. Beds so neat they can bounce pennies off the sheets.

Gladys, now thirty-six, rents an apartment; Jamie, thirty-eight, lives in a house. Staying with their mother, and with the kids they'd spent sixteen years away from, turned out to be difficult for them both. Their own children spoke to them any kind of way—*Don't tell us what to do. You didn't raise us.*

Meanwhile their mother wanted to do everything for them. Get their Social Security cards, their birth certificates. No, Jamie and Gladys would tell her; just show us. We can do it. During their first week in Pensacola, they stopped at a Walmart. Greeters rushed up to them. Crowds jammed the aisles. People were swiping their credit cards at the cash register, talking into cell phones. Jamie started hyperventilating. It was all too fast.

Jamie and Gladys were both born in Chicago's Cook County Hospital. They grew up on the fifteenth floor of a housing project at 44th Street and South Cottage Grove, surrounded by gang fights and shootings, never knowing when they might step over a body. One day, when Jamie was twelve, the elevator in their building opened to reveal a dead man abandoned inside. She screamed, and her father rushed her back into their apartment. She saw children fall from windows high above the ground when they leaned out too far throwing water balloons. She saw shootings, stabbings. After a while, death no longer shocked. Jamie and Gladys learned to be cautious. Anything could happen, and they had no control over it when it did.

Their father was a maintenance supervisor at the University of Illinois. He had a side job too; he'd take janitorial supplies from the university hospital and use them to clean houses. When no one noticed, he started taking other hospital equipment and selling it. Eventually the man he did this with was caught and ratted James out, but the hospital couldn't prove his involvement. The hospital gave James the option to retire after twenty years, and he took it. He told his family he was taking them to Mississippi; he was going to get them away from Chicago's violence and look after his elderly parents. His mother had developed the beginnings of Alzheimer's disease. She was still well enough, when they got to Hillsboro, to tell Jamie and Gladys that the Rascos had always been into illegal occupations. James, she said, comes from a long line of people who did things outside the law to make money.

The family moved into a three-bedroom house owned by James's parents. At first, Gladys and Jamie hated Hillsboro's slow pace; they missed their Chicago friends, and they promised themselves that once they turned eighteen they would return to the city. Before they could do that, however, they'd gotten pregnant and dropped out of high school. They stayed in Hillsboro. Jamie had had one son already, before they'd moved south; in Hillsboro she gave birth to another son and one daughter before having her tubes tied in November 1993. Gladys had a daughter after their move, and was pregnant with a second daughter when the robbery occurred, at the end of that year. By then their father had opened the Sugar Hill nightclub. Hillsboro is part of Scott County, a dry county; James bought booze in Jackson and sold it from the Sugar Hill. He hired girls from Chicago and paid them to strip on weekends.

Jamie and Gladys knew what their father was up to, but no one in the family discussed it. He was the world to them; he took care of them, and they never went without. They'd disappointed him when they'd decided to quit school. He could neither read nor write, and he'd wanted them to get their diplomas. Anticipating her graduation, he'd even paid for Jamie's class ring. He was strong-willed and hot-tempered. He didn't trust banks and kept his money buried in the woods. He knew the woods well. And he knew how to make a dollar.

After the girls had given up on school, James put Jamie to work in his club, cooking. By 10 a.m., he told her, I want you to cut up five onions and two bell peppers. Put them on the grill and turn it low. Within minutes, when people heard the sizzling and smelled the aromas rising from the kitchen, they'd start ordering catfish plates, hamburger plates, rib plates with fries and baked beans. Sometimes Jamie helped the club bring in several hundred dollars a day. Gladys helped too, but neither of them served liquor. James handled that. The police knew what he was doing, but James paid them off.

At some point some Mississippi guys began selling crack outside the club. Eventually one of them was shot there, and the police closed the place down for a few weeks. When the club reopened, the drug dealers were gone, and James had decided to get in on their action. He began supplying crack to Scott and Jasper counties. His daughters were terrified, worried that their father would get arrested. The police raided their house and found dope in the refrigerator. James paid them off again.

After a while the police wanted more money. James refused,

and that's when all the trouble started. Miss Evelyn began complaining that the police were following her to bingo. If they get behind you, don't stop, James told her. Get to the house and blow your horn and I'll handle it from there.

By then Jamie had left the club and was working at a chicken plant, cutting chicken tenders eight hours a day. She didn't see a future for herself at her father's place. She knew how it would end.

On the night of December 23, 1993, the heater in Jamie's Hillsboro house died. Gladys dropped by, and Jamie told her she needed to find the gasman, Ken. It was after hours, but Jamie knew that Ken drove the gas truck home; people would pay him on the side to fill their tanks.

The sisters took Jamie's car to Ken's house, but Ken was out with friends. Jamie left a note with Ken's wife, then drove to a mini-mart in Forest to put gas in the car. When they'd filled it up, though, the car wouldn't start. That was when Gladys saw two men she knew, Johnny Ray Hayes and Mitchell Duckworth, and offered to pay them ten dollars for a ride home.

Jamie got in the backseat with Duckworth; it was Johnny's car. It was getting close to 10 p.m., the night cold and clear. Duckworth began making advances, Jamie says—he asked her name, and offered to give her $300 to come with him to a hotel.

I don't sleep around, you hear me? Jamie told him.

When they passed the Cow Pasture, another nightclub, Jamie saw a cousin of theirs and asked Hayes to stop. She got out and asked her cousin if he could run them home, but he told her he was waiting on some dope. Jamie got back in the car.

Duckworth started hitting on her again, pulling on her arm. When he ripped her shirt, Jamie started screaming for Hayes to stop the car again. She and Gladys got out, she says; they were near their father's house, and they started walking. Hayes and Duckworth shouted after them, calling them bitches. Jamie glanced back, she says, and saw another car approaching Hayes's, but thought little of it.

Around midnight, some friends stopped by Jamie's house. They told her they'd had a confrontation on Cow Pasture Road with a couple of "dudes"; the men they described sounded like Hayes and Duckworth. Jamie's friends said they'd taken some beer and demanded money, but the dudes hadn't had any.

The next morning, Christmas Eve, Jamie was lying on the couch in her front room, still sore from her November operation. Her mother stood in her kitchen, preparing Christmas dinner. Evelyn had run out of room in her own kitchen, so she'd come over to put a ham in Jamie's oven. Moments after she left, the Scott County sheriff showed up. He told Jamie that she and Gladys were being arrested for robbing Hayes and Duckworth.

Do I look like I robbed somebody? Jamie said as they hand-cuffed her. Her children were screaming. Her three-year-old son ran after the squad car as it drove away until he collapsed in the dirt, crying.

Jamie says the sheriff told her that if she and Gladys revealed her father's drug connections, they would be home by Christmas. She and Gladys refused to say anything. The charges, Jamie says, were then upgraded to armed robbery. Enoch McCurdy says people in Hillsboro are still shocked that the Scott sisters were arrested. Nobody believed it at first.

Enoch, sixty, a nephew of James Rasco, didn't. He knew James was dealing drugs at the time. James had told Enoch that he wasn't going to pay the sheriff anything. The arrests drove James crazy, Enoch says. He grieved for his imprisoned daughters. He broke down. His hair turned gray, and he lost weight. He spent hundreds of dollars on bribes to get Jamie and Gladys off, but it wasn't going to happen. That's how it goes in Mississippi.

Olivia Flake is twenty-three now. She was seven when her mother, Gladys, was sent to prison. Evelyn took her to visit Gladys every other Sunday; at first they could sit with Gladys in her cell, but then they started meeting her in a big open-space visiting center, with food and snack machines and a soda dispenser. Sodas cost two dollars. There was a photo booth too. Olivia's younger sister was born in 1994. Prison officials took Gladys to the University of Mississippi Medical Center when she went into labor. She was chained to a bed and allowed just two days with her newborn daughter before she was told to turn the child over to her mother or to the state. Gladys let Evelyn take the baby and let Olivia choose a name. Olivia decided on Courtney, the name of a close friend.

After a few years, visiting the prison twice a month seemed normal. Oh, our mom is in prison—like, Oh, our mom's at the mall. Olivia didn't write many letters to her mother. She didn't want this you-have-to-write-your-mother-because-she's-in-prison thing going on. When she was thirteen, Olivia gave birth to a boy of her own and named him Xander, a Greek word that means "protector of men." She liked the strength of the name, the sense of security it gave her. She had run away by then and wanted to do her own thing. She felt lost. Miss Evelyn took care of Xander for her.

Olivia wants to be close to Gladys, but doesn't know if she can. It's awkward, trying to do the mother-daughter thing. She doesn't feel motivated. Recently she met a man through the internet, Ozondu Duru. He lives in Nigeria. Olivia thinks she loves him; she's applied for a passport and plans to move there to be with him. She wants to get married.

The morning the jury announced its verdict, Gladys had a premonition that she was not going home. She'd seen one of the jurors putting on makeup during the trial, like she wasn't even listening. The trial lasted two days. Seven white and five black jurors deliberated for half an hour before coming to a decision. Jamie and Gladys were each found guilty of two counts of armed robbery. Mississippi law permits juries to recommend a life sentence for armed robbery, so each sister received two life sentences, one for each armed-robbery count. Both girls collapsed after the guards escorted them from the courtroom. Double life sentence. Because of their father, Gladys thought. She could see the look on his face as the verdict was read, the disbelief, the hurt in his eyes.

Gladys and Jamie were held in the Scott County Jail for two more days before being transported to the Central Mississippi Correctional Facility in Rankin, where they were booked, fingerprinted, and escorted to a shower room. They stood with the other new women in a circle, the water crashing down on their bodies as the male guards watched. Several of the women there had already been in the prison three or four times; they told Jamie and Gladys to mind their own business and not get in anyone's way.

New inmates sentenced to fifteen years or more were put on

suicide watch in solitary confinement before they were released into the general population. Gladys and Jamie were placed in twelve-by-twelve-foot cells, each one with a steel bed attached to the wall, a sink, and a toilet. A guard slid their food through a slot in the door. If it fell off the tray, oh well.

They spoke to other inmates by screaming under their doors. They talked to each other through a vent by the toilets. Jamie entered the general population within six months; Gladys remained in solitary longer, because she'd argued with a guard. Even when she was released to general population, she stayed angry. Little things ticked her off. When an inmate tried to take her turn in the shower, she fought back. She always stayed alert. Anyone who spoke to her, no matter how nice, might be messing with her head. They might like her one day and try to hurt her the next. If she slipped up, she'd be seen as weak. She'd be run over.

Sometimes the guards would shake down her cell, tear up letters, photos of her children. She would just stand there, silent. As time passed, however, Gladys did get close to some of them. Hard not to, seeing them every day, year after year. They would tell her about their problems in the free world. But the good ones always left.

The last thirty days in prison were the hardest, Gladys says. The last week was worse than the first. She was snappy, irritable. She wanted to get out. When the day arrived, January 7, 2011, Gladys started shaking. She was wearing a two-piece purple dress suit, purple earrings, and a pair of purple high heels. The shoes were too big, and it took her a moment to manage to walk in them. The sisters had been told by other inmates that if they looked back when they left, they would return to prison.

They wanted to look back, to see the women they'd spent sixteen years with one last time, but they were afraid.

Nearly a year later, Gladys shifts on her couch and gives her walls an unblinking, thousand-mile stare. Christmas is just weeks away. She and Jamie were arrested in December; she worries about a knock on her door, an expressionless officer telling her it's time to come with him. Do as much time as she has, and that fear is going to be with you for a minute. Gladys and Jamie have midnight curfews. They cannot travel beyond Pensacola without permission. They cannot drink alcohol. They report to a probation officer once a month, and will do so for the remainder of their lives unless they receive a pardon. Their parole officer can drop by anytime, night or day. Demand a piss test. Search the house.

Gladys's cell phone rings. A woman she knew in prison who just got out.

Your momma happy you home? Gladys says. I bet she is, girl. Can't sleep, can you? Three or four days without it, uh-huh. What'd you eat when you got out? I gained my weight back. I'm big as a hat.

The Scott County district attorney agreed with the Scott sisters' version of events, up to a point. They did, the DA said, ask Johnny Ray Hayes and Mitchell Duckworth for a ride home from the mini-mart in Forest. On the way back to Hillsboro, they did stop at the Cow Pasture. But then, the DA claimed, Gladys asked to drive.

According to the prosecution, they stopped next at a house in Forest, where the sisters spoke to someone in a blue Oldsmobile. Afterward, Gladys continued driving; when Jamie complained of feeling ill, Gladys slowed to a stop. Another car came up behind them then, and a man with a shotgun robbed Hayes and Duckworth. Hayes claimed he turned over "about two- hundred-something dollars." Duckworth said he "didn't have much money in [his] wallet. Really nothing, probably." Hayes said that Jamie and Gladys left with the robbers.

Howard Patrick, fourteen, and his cousin Gregory Patrick, eighteen, testified against the Scott sisters as part of a plea deal they'd worked out for themselves. Howard said that he and Gregory, along with Howard's sixteen-year-old brother, Christopher, had committed the robbery. They were friends of the Scott sisters, he said; on the night in question, they'd met the girls at the mini-mart, and Gladys had conceived of the holdup. Howard's share of the stolen money was "nine, ten, eleven dollars." During the trial, Howard Patrick admitted that he hadn't bothered to read the statement that had implicated the Scott sisters before he signed it. It had been given to him by the sheriff's department.

> Q: And you had been promised that if you signed the statement, you could get out of jail the next morning?
>
> A: That, and they said if I didn't participate with them, they would send me to Parchman [Mississippi State Penitentiary] and make me out a female.
>
> Q: I'm sorry?
>
> A: That they would let me out of jail the next

morning, and that if I didn't participate with them, that they would send me to Parchman and make me out a female.

Q: In other words, they would send you to Parchman, and you would get raped, right?

A: Yes, sir.

Q: So you decided it was better to sign the statement, even without reading it?

A: I didn't know what it was.

Sixty-two-year-old Willy Tooks, of Hillsboro, did not testify at the trial, but he would have had something to say had he been asked. He was in the Scott County Jail at the same time as the Patrick boys, after the robbery. Tooks had shoplifted a ham from a Sunflower supermarket in Forest. Those boys, he says, were talking about Jamie and Gladys—talking about how they were going to give state's evidence against them. They were smoking cigarettes and just talking. They were going to try to get a lighter sentence. At the time, Tooks didn't think one way or the other about it. He wanted to get out of jail his own self.

Celestine Lewis directs the Jacqueline Harris Preparatory Academy, a Pensacola charter school where Jamie holds a clerical job. In January 2011, Miss Lewis, as everyone calls her, read about the Scott sisters' release from prison in the newspaper and about their move to Pensacola. Sixteen years incarcerated, she recalls thinking at the time. Sixteen years and then released into this big old mean world. Oh God, I'd like to see these girls enrich their lives, she thought. Her mother died a few days later. She needed something to take her mind off it.

Miss Lewis called the Scotts' mother and asked to speak with Jamie and Gladys. I don't want anything, Miss Lewis told her. I just want to meet you-all. At a Red Lobster where she took them for lunch, Miss Lewis explained how tipping worked. She told Jamie and Gladys to keep their left hands on their laps and not to eat like they had nothing and to use a napkin.

We didn't have napkins in prison, and we had to eat in fifteen minutes, Jamie told her. Sometimes you only had five minutes to eat. You ate what you could and threw away the rest. We had to be in the cafeteria by 5:40 in the morning. Every day we ate oatmeal, potatoes, gravy and biscuits. Lunch was bologna, dinner was spaghetti. Sometimes you'd bite into a bug but you didn't complain because you didn't want to go to solitary. You just sat there and chewed on that bug.

Miss Lewis told Jamie and Gladys she grew up in a shotgun house. You could see straight through it like a tunnel. Her mother and father did not graduate from high school. Her father was a laborer. Her mother pushed education. The Lord first, then education, she'd say. If you don't have both, you're doomed.

Girls, napkins on your lap, please.

A new lawyer, Chokwe Lumumba, represented the Scott sisters on appeal. He contacted Chris Patrick, the only one of the Patrick boys not to testify during the original trial. Chris swore in a signed affidavit that Jamie and Gladys had not been involved in the robbery.

> Prior to the trial of Gladys and Jamie Scott, Deputy Marvin Williams of the Scott County Sheriff Department told me and my brother Howard in my presence that we would serve life sentences in Parchman Prison if we did not agree to testify against Gladys and Jamie Scott, and if we did not agree to testify that both women took part in planning for and setting up the robbery of Duckworth and Hayes.

Lumumba found other individuals who raised questions about the case as well. Willie Shepard, who worked as a trustee at the Scott County Jail at the time of the robbery, said that a few days afterward, he and a few other prisoners were taken to the scene by sheriff's deputies in order to search for evidence. One trustee discovered Duckworth's wallet with three twenty-dollar bills in it.

"Duckworth was one of the alleged victims of the alleged robbery," Shepard told Lumumba. "[Deputy] Marvin [Murls] knew Duckworth, because he lived near his family. Once we were back at the jail, Marvin called all of us trustees together. Marvin said, looking directly at me, 'If this gets back to Hillsboro, you are going to ride Buddy's truck.' He meant he was going to send me to Parchman." Lumumba believed that in order to prop up the robbery story, the deputy had wanted to conceal that money had been left at the scene.

Lumumba's appeal was denied. Next he petitioned then governor Ronnie Musgrove for a commutation of the Scott sisters' sentence. He noted that the Patricks had already been released from prison.

"Remember," Lumumba wrote, "neither Gladys nor Jamie had any prior convictions or arrests. There was no murder or even hospitalization of the alleged victims in this case. Therefore the question becomes whether these two women should have been sentenced to such harsh punishments for crimes that they clearly did not commit."

The commutation request was denied.

Sixteen years.

James Rasco died in 2003. In 2004, Evelyn Rasco's mother died too. Jamie and Gladys's older sister Evelyn, named after their mother, died of congestive heart failure in 2008. And then, in 2010, Jamie's kidneys began to fail.

Gladys helps her eight-year-old niece, Shamira, the daughter of her sister Evelyn, with her homework. Gladys and Jamie share the responsibility of raising Shamira now. Until recently Gladys was also in school, attending classes at Pensacola State College. She received her GED in December, but now she's decided to take a semester off, the better to look after her mother. In the meantime she wants to find work at a nursing home. Something stable. When an employer realizes that the gaps in her work history are a result of time served in prison, she worries that the application will go into the garbage. Right now she has a job at a barbecue joint for three hours a day. Members of her church knew the owner, and recommended her. Sometimes, as Gladys works in the kitchen, her mind drifts back to her job in the prison cafeteria. She remembers the big pots. Big enough to sit in. Gladys, come back, her boss at the barbecue joint says, and the memory pops like a soap bubble.

Finding an apartment was another challenge. No one

wanted to rent to an ex-felon. Eventually she found a landlord who didn't bother with background checks. She told him her story anyway, to be on the level. As long as you never molested children, he told her. Gladys assured him that she had not.

At Pensacola State, Gladys worked in an administrative office. One morning a secretary noticed a copy of *Ebony* jutting out of Gladys's bag and asked to read it. Gladys gave it to her, and the secretary leafed through it until she reached an article about the Scott sisters' release. She glanced at Gladys, who had just answered a phone.

Kind of cold in here, Gladys said after she'd hung up. Must have the air on high.

I heard about you on the news, the secretary said. They really did that? Said it was you and your sister's idea to rob them boys?

Yes, Gladys said. She started stuffing GED forms into folders.

You went through a lot. Why didn't you say anything?

Didn't know how you'd treat me, Gladys said. Some people treat you different when they know you've been in prison.

I wouldn't have.

How would I know that? Gladys said.

There was this older lady Jamie knew inside, Miss Alberta. Seventy-something. Murdered her husband. Life sentence. She told Jamie, If you find yourself not eating or bathing and your hair coming out, you'll find yourself in the grave. You got to keep hope. Read the Bible. Don't let your time be idle.

Gladys was friends with an inmate named Angel. Angel loved to dance. She was a little slow, and would get into it with the guards. Gladys combed her hair, helped her with makeup.

When Angel was a child, her stepfather sold her for crack. Angel was released while Gladys and Jamie were incarcerated, but she was back inside within twenty-four hours. She had tried to kill her stepfather for molesting her son.

Gladys was working in the kitchen, and brought food to her. She saw Angel hanging by the vent in her cell. Gladys kicked the door and screamed—Get her down! Get her down! But she was already dead.

Jamie's son Richard was eleven months old when his mother was arrested. His grandmother described her to him; he didn't remember her. Where is she now? he would ask. Out of town, she said.

When he went to visit his mother for the first time, Richard thought his grandparents had taken him to a zoo—the walls, the wire fence. He didn't know who his mother was when he saw her. She picked him up on the prison playground; he remembers how strong she was. When it was time to go, it was hard to leave. He thought this woman who was his mother was very nice. He remembers that Jamie and Gladys both attended his grandfather's funeral. James had told Richard that it was his responsibility as a man to watch out for his girl cousins. He'd taught him about farming corn, cabbage, beans, potatoes, pecans, about hunting deer and boar. He'd urged Richard to get an education.

Evelyn, Richard's aunt, was strict with him. He loved her for it. She would help him with his math and reading, and he would help her when she wrote letters on behalf of Jamie and Gladys. When she lost a page somewhere, he'd rummage through the house to find it. She would stay up late writing, and he would help her to bed. It hurts now, seeing her in the hospital.

Richard was thirteen, maybe fourteen, when Evelyn died. He remembers his mother at the funeral in a black-and-white prison jumpsuit, wrapped in chains. Aunt Gladys was in solitary then, and not allowed to attend. It was a hot day. Not cloudy. Two guards stood beside Richard's mother; they moved back some when she went to stand by the grave. After the funeral everyone walked into the church cafeteria. Jamie had to eat, because of her diabetes. The guards waited at the cafeteria doors. They told Jamie, You got two minutes.

It surprises Pastor Lonnie D. Wesley of the Greater Little Rock Baptist Church what Jamie and Gladys don't know. When Gladys was in a car accident, neither she nor Jamie knew to call the police or their insurance company. They called Pastor Wesley instead. Things like that aren't trivial, he says. At one point, Jamie told Pastor Wesley that she wanted to return to prison. Life outside was too confusing. In prison, she knew what was expected of her. The guards trusted her. New inmates respected her. She didn't have to worry about light bills, gas bills, car accidents. But then she thought of her mother and Shamira, and knew she wouldn't be able to do anything for either of them if she went back to being locked up.

Pastor Wesley has concluded that a level of comfort exists in prison. The regimentation allows for no uncertainty. No one will have a car accident in prison. An ex-felon has to think in new ways. So when Jamie and Gladys call Pastor Wesley for help, he does not respond immediately. He waits a few days, affords them the grace to make mistakes. They would not learn otherwise. They will learn only by making choices despite the pain and uncertainty.

It's all about want-to, Pastor Wesley believes. Gladys and Jamie have the want-to. Even when they make mistakes. Even when they panic. It's the want-to that keeps mistakes and panic from being detrimental.

Evelyn Rasco lies in a bed at Pensacola's Baptist Hospital, asleep. A nurse places a blanket over her. Miss Evelyn, sixty-five, has not been eating. Her weight has dropped from 250 to 119 pounds in three months. Doctors worry about malnutrition. It seems so unfair to her family, that she would be so sick now, when Jamie and Gladys are finally out.

Miss Evelyn left Hillsboro in 2000, taking Jamie's and Gladys's five children with her. She had a son in the army in Pensacola, and she needed to get away from James and his lifestyle. Once she settled in Florida, Miss Evelyn began writing letters to community activists, law schools—anyone she thought might help free her daughters. She only had an eighth-grade education but expressed herself clearly and forcefully. She budgeted money for stamps and ink cartridges.

In the fall of 2005 she wrote to Jesse Jackson's son, Congressman Jesse Jackson III. Her letter was passed on to the elder Jackson's Rainbow PUSH coalition and came to the attention of Nancy Lockhart, a law student at Loyola University in Chicago and a community services consultant at Rainbow PUSH. Included with the letter was a six-page booklet Jamie had put together about the case. If Rainbow PUSH could not help her, Miss Evelyn had written, please recommend another agency that might. No fluff, Lockhart recalls now. Direct and to the point.

Lockhart began to work with Miss Evelyn to draw attention to the case. Progress was slow; Rainbow PUSH and other organizations like it seemed reluctant to get involved. In 2008,

Lockhart began using the internet to spread the Scott sisters' story; she filed guest posts for web magazines and started her own website, wrongfulconvictions.wordpress.com. Soon *Mother Jones* and the *New York Times* were raising questions about the case. By 2009, Lockhart became convinced that the State of Mississippi was going to have to do something.

Jamie sits in the waiting room of the dialysis center at Fresenius Medical Care in Pensacola's Cordova Mall, waiting for the receptionist to call her name.

You been on yet? another patient asks her.

No. Just got here.

Jamie was diagnosed with diabetes in 2003, when her gallbladder was removed. In 2010, her bloodwork showed that she'd gone into complete renal failure and would have to be placed on dialysis. Shortly after that, a guard told Gladys to speak to Jamie. Jamie knew nothing about dialysis and had refused treatment. She would die without it, the guard said.

You're not leaving me, Gladys told her. We lost one sister while we've been here. I don't want to lose another. We walk out the way we came in, together. The trailer housing the dialysis machine at the prison was filthy. Mold grew on the outside of it, and dust covered the floor. Two male nurses and four female nurses connected patients to the machines. Jamie was struck by their smiles. No hint of judgment. You might as well stop looking like it's the end of the world, a male nurse would joke with her. You're too pretty.

The dialysis treatment takes about four hours, three times a week. Jamie can't describe the feeling of her blood being pumped out of and back into her body. Weird. Like a steady stream going through you. Would a man want me if he knew I had health problems? Jamie wonders. Would he accept me?

She would cook for him and try to be as normal as possible, but would it be enough? Would he look at her the way Gladys does? That look of, Lord, please don't let my sister die.

She needs to lose more than one hundred pounds before she'll be eligible for a kidney transplant. If Gladys's kidney isn't a match, Jamie will be put on a waiting list. Gladys will then donate a kidney to someone else, as required by the conditions of her parole.

To lose weight, Jamie exercises at the Pensacourt Sports Center three or four times a week. She runs, lifts weights, and rides a stationary bicycle in a yellow-brick room she calls the torture room. When she finishes her exercise, her trainer goes over her diet.

What'd you have yesterday?

Gladys cooked greens. No fatback. Turkey, bacon, sweet potatoes.

What's on the sweet potatoes?

Nothing. I ate two boiled eggs and one of my protein things. Didn't have a snack. Chicken for lunch.

You stopped drinking soda?

Yes.

Good. Lots of regular water?

Yes.

Obstacles?

My momma is in the hospital. It's depressing. A woman who fought so hard for us and she don't want to fight for herself, it seems like. My mind is focused on that. I've been hungry.

It's a stressful time. Stay on track.

In December 2010, Jamie and Gladys knew the governor was considering a pardon. Members of the pardon board had spoken to them in the middle of the month. If you're released, where would you go, what would you do? What would you say to the governor, if you could talk to him?

The pardon board did not want to hear them declare their innocence. They weren't considering their innocence. They were considering whether they should be released. Jamie and Gladys told them the governor would never have to worry that he'd made the wrong decision. They would not return to jail. They were not criminals.

Their release was announced on December 27. Governor Barbour said he based his decision in part on a desire to relieve the state of the cost of Jamie's dialysis treatment—about $200,000 a year. Johnny Ray Hayes and Mitchell Duckworth have never commented publicly on the Scott sisters' case. The men have never attempted to contact them. Neither have the Patricks. Just as well, Jamie and Gladys say. Those boys put them away for sixteen years.

Jamie and Gladys awaken and feel blessed.

Small things please them. Opening their refrigerators and seeing food they bought themselves. Sitting on couches they can call their own. A rug at Gladys's feet shows children praying. She and Jamie prayed like that at their grandmother Big Momma's urging.

They returned to Hillsboro once to attend the birthday of their ninety-six-year-old auntie, and stayed with a cousin. Jamie rarely left the house. She didn't trust anything about Forest and Hillsboro. She and Gladys did visit their father's grave across from the Sylvester Methodist Church. It was hard for them to think of him underground. Is he really in there? Jamie had asked herself. He had been so strong and had such an influence—good and bad—on their lives.

Sometimes, when they have nothing to do, they contemplate the sky and the trees and the way branches sway even when there's no wind, and how falling leaves drift from one side to the other until they dip and spiral to the ground. At other times, they might cry for no reason. Or they might space out driving and pull over and wonder, How did I wind up here?

Every morning, they bolt out of bed and stand ready for the inspection that will not come, knowing somewhere deep beneath the clamor of a prison dream fading from their minds that they're home now. They can close their bedroom doors.

Can't nobody see them. Can't nobody write them up. Can't nobody come in.

A Product of This Town

Outsiders, all of you. Your presence here is a judgment on us. It was worse in September 2007, when thousands of you descended with the indignation of embittered preachers. Businesses shut down. People stayed home behind locked doors. The silence of those days still lingers, still carries a warning of approaching tumult.

We pray for the people who come to Jena. God loves them no matter what their agenda, although we feel their agenda is misplaced. We pray for our community to be patient. We pray for everything to be back to normal.

Your judgment was felt on this January night in the year of our Lord 2008, by boys looping Oak Street, trolling endlessly up and down and through the center of town. Cruising, you would call it, but in Jena, it's called "looping." The loop starts in the darkened parking lot of Champlin's Furniture, where teenagers sit in their idling pickups and lean out their windows, talking on weekend nights. Boys mostly. Some with their arms draped around their girlfriends. Then, as if by migratory compulsion, they slip their gears into drive and turn east through the unlit, empty streets. The boys roll past the Dollar General store, Ace Family Hardware, and McDonald's, where a teenager hands a sack of burgers out the drive-through window. A light illuminates the State Farm insurance sign. A dog caught in its thin glow lopes past silent display windows. Brandon's Nails, Reid's Jewelry store, Honeycutt Drug.

Those white boys acted and we reacted. I'm just saying that's the way things happen in this little town.

Three minutes from Champlin's the boys turn into the parking lot of Mitch's Restaurant (*Today's Special: the catfish plate*) and complete the loop. They pause, adjust their radios, and then retrace their steps like panthers in a cage, back and forth, back and forth all night.

That used to be the whole, limited journey. But lately it seems the loop has expanded, as if some of the youngsters kept going, looping the whole damn country, and then pulling it with them each time they turned back to Jena. More of you keep coming. And still the loop gets bigger.

Some of you-all have returned this week for the Martin Luther King birthday march on Sunday, haven't you? You know about the protest by those fellas with the Nationalist Movement, right? A real party, yeah, buddy. Will there be fights? Will blood run? You'll tar and feather Jena for your own sport, won't you?

It's about where we're at. The South. This is being done to us because of geographics. We're the South, so outsiders say Jena's a racist town.

What is so different about Jena from your town?

What god made you judge and jury?

Just who are you, anyway?

In September 2006, nooses were hung from a tree in the high school courtyard in Jena, Louisiana. The tree was on the side of campus that, by long-standing tradition, had always been claimed by white students, who make up more than 80 percent of the student body. But a few of the school's eighty-five black students had decided to challenge the status quo by pointing out their de facto exclusion: they asked the school administrators if they, too, could sit beneath the tree's cooling shade. The nooses were hung in retaliation, as a kind of threat.

Three white students were quickly identified as responsible, and the principal recommended that they be expelled. But Jena's school superintendent, Roy Breithaupt, who is white, intervened and ruled that the nooses were just an immature stunt. He suspended the students for three days, angering those who felt harsher punishments were necessary. Racial tensions flared throughout the month, and on November 30 a wing of the high school was destroyed by a fire; officials suspected arson. Tensions spilled out of the schoolyard and into the surrounding neighborhoods. One night at a predominantly white party, a young black student was assaulted by a group wielding beer bottles. In another incident, a white Jena graduate allegedly pulled a pump-action shotgun on three black students outside a local convenience store. The teens managed to wrestle the gun away from the twenty-one-year-old.

For the most part, local law enforcement stayed out of the way of these incidents, shrugging them off as testosterone-fueled teenage arguments. This approach shifted abruptly on December 4—more than a month after the black students sat under the "white" tree—when a fight broke out in the lunchroom between a white student and a black student. The white student was knocked to the floor and allegedly attacked by other black students, one of whom was the same student assaulted earlier at the party. The white student sustained bruises and a black eye. He was treated at a hospital and released. According to court testimony, he attended a social event later that same evening.

The black students were not reprimanded with school suspensions or misdemeanor charges, as their white counterparts had been. Instead, five of the six black teens involved were charged as adults with attempted second-degree murder and were given bonds ranging from $70,000 to $138,000. Sixteen-year-old Mychal Bell was prosecuted as an adult and assigned a public defender, a black man, who never called a single witness. Under pressure by watchdog groups, the district attorney abruptly reduced the charges against Bell from second-degree murder to second-degree aggravated battery and conspiracy. The charge of aggravated battery stems from the prosecutor's contention that the teens' gym shoes were used as weapons.

Donald Washington, a black U.S. attorney for the Western District of Louisiana, insisted race had nothing to do with the charges against Bell. He said that the hanging of nooses constituted a hate crime, but that charges were not brought against those students because they were juveniles. Washington was unable to explain, however, why Bell was prosecuted as an adult by a white prosecutor. While teenagers can be tried as adults in Louisiana for some violent crimes, including attempted murder, aggravated battery is not one of those crimes. An appeals court tossed out the conviction that could have sent him to prison for fifteen years. But the four remaining students, who could be tried as adults because they were seventeen or older, were arraigned on battery and conspiracy charges.

In response to the treatment of "the Jena Six," more than five thousand protesters converged on Jena last September to express their outrage. The scene was reminiscent of a 1960s freedom march, and many of those old-school leaders, including Reverends Jesse Jackson and Al Sharpton, were in attendance. But there were also some new faces. Young faces. All excited to play a part in what some of them called "our Selma."

White supremacists did their part to evoke their 1960s counterparts as well. "The best crowd control for such a situation would be a squad of men armed with full automatics and preferably a machine gun as well," advocated an online blogger on the neo-Nazi Vanguard News Network. Another wrote, "I'm not really that angry at the nogs—they are just soldiers in an undeclared race war. But any white that's in that support rally I would like to . . . have them machine-gunned." Bill White, an especially virulent purveyor of race hate, posted the home addresses and phone numbers of some of the Jena Six under this headline: "Addresses of Jena 6 Niggers: In Case Anyone Wants to Deliver Justice."

My drive to Jena started on Saturday, January 19, 2008—four days after MLK's birthday—and took me through Little Rock, Arkansas, where I picked up a copy of the *Arkansas Democrat-Gazette*. On the editorial page, an article celebrated the birthday of Robert E. Lee ("It is January 19th again, Lee's birthday, now an official holiday in this state").

I was going to Jena in time to see the Martin Luther King birthday march, though I'd been warned that the Mississippi-based white supremacist Nationalist Movement was planning to disrupt the MLK march by demonstrating on the same day. The mostly black high school marching band had already dropped out as parents became more and more concerned about safety. At the last minute, the march was moved to Sunday, January 20, a day before King's official celebration, to avoid conflict with the Nationalist Movement's Monday rally. Beth Rickey, the spokeswoman for Jena's mayor, told me that Jena had been turned into an armed camp of plainclothes cops anticipating a clash between the groups.

Before I left for Jena, I learned some history. The town was settled in 1802. Benjamin Baker and his father built a water mill for cornmeal and gin cotton about three miles below the present town of Jena. A post office was named for another family of early settlers, the Hemphills.

Between 1882 and 1965, more than 330 people, all black, were lynched in Louisiana—more than four a year. When Klan leader David Duke ran for governor of Louisiana in 1991, spouting antiblack and anti-Jewish slurs, the vast majority of Jena voted for him.

I pull into Hughey Leggett's driveway just outside the Jena city limits. He is sipping a beer on the porch of his wood-frame house, which is a shrine to his dead brother, the country singer Johnny Leggett. A tiny bandstand is crowded with drums and cymbals, a small PA system, photos of Johnny. Dogs gambol in the yard beneath a Confederate flag. Leggett once had the Stars and Stripes but took it down. No particular reason. Louisiana is a Confederate state, Leggett tells me, as if that is explanation enough. He's been to Jena a bunch of times. Lots of whites and blacks. They all seem to get along. As long as they're involved in their own business and don't stir nothing up, everything's fine. No problems except last fall, when Jesse Jackson and that Al Sharpton came here. They can't win the presidency so they go around the country and cause trouble. You have a scab on your finger, scratch it and it starts bleeding. Those two, they've been doing some serious scratching. Caused some bleeding, they have. He sips his beer and says no more.

Down at a ramshackle club called the Yellow Cat, cigarette smoke froths the stale air above the heads of black men. The building is basically a barn, thick with cobwebs and faded beer signs. An old jukebox hums with 45s: Bobby Bland ("I Just Tripped on a Piece of Your Broken Heart"), Johnnie Taylor ("Good Love"), Billy Ray Charles ("What's Your Pleasure").

"Hear there's going to be another march."

"Ain't surprised."

"Nothing in Jena surprises me."

"Remember that black guy killed in '64?"

"The shoe shop guy?"

"He made too much money as far as white folks was concerned."

"Is it sleeting outside?"

"Raining. A bit."

"'64, '04, makes no difference what year we in."

"It's 2008, fool."

"Like I said, makes no difference. Damn this weather."

Bernice Coleman Mack leans forward on her walker while a home health nurse braids her hair. Her grandson, Robert Bailey, is one of the Jena Six. She suspects the Devil's hand behind all this trouble. Old man Satan is busy going to and fro seeing who he can tempt. She doesn't know why it all happened. The noose-hangers heard they used to hang black folk. That's why they put up those ropes. A signal. If you do anything wrong, you'll hang. If they read scripture they would know better. Something went wrong, but she doesn't know what. At eighty-four, her face a canyon of wrinkles etched with worry, she knows a thing or two. Satan, she says again.

My mother and father hail from Cuba and Puerto Rico, respectively, but through the mysteries of genetics, I look as white as most Caucasians. As a boy, I would hear my friends' parents discuss their dislike of minorities. I stopped introducing myself as Malcolm Garcia. I just said "Malcolm." Without my troublesome last name, I could "pass," but that never made me comfortable; I was always on the edge—both inside the white world and outside it.

In 1997, I took a job in Philadelphia. I used to eat at a diner down the street from my apartment. One afternoon, I sat next to a man in a suit and tie, and we began exchanging pleasantries as we ate. I introduced myself and he paused, mouth open, full of partially eaten hamburger.

"Malcolm," he said, repeating my name. "Your parents liberal?"

"What do you mean?"

"Why else would they name you after Malcolm X?"

I told him I wasn't named for Malcolm X, that my last name was Garcia.

"Garcia?" he asked. "You got a little color in you, don't you, boy?"

I approach the people of Jena with caution.

Pastors joke that eleven o'clock Mass in Jena's thirteen churches is the most segregated hour of the week. Some black people have told white Pentecostal pastor Eddie Thompson they would attend his church, but they haven't. And there are no white people attending the services of Reverend B. L. Moran at Antioch Baptist Church in the unincorporated side of Jena,

called Ward 10, once referred to by whites as "the quarters."
Two white men ran over his sign after an NAACP meeting last
year. Drove a big old mail truck over it twice. Said it was an
accident; they were just turning around.

Reverend Thompson calls that sort of thing "stealth racism."
You got some hotheads and knotheads, he says. Children of racism
that have stained Jena and put the town up as a sacrifice on the
racial altar of America. The country has not dealt with the spirit
and hatred still lurking within. How, he asks, can we move forward
if the heart has not been opened? America didn't transcend racism
during some march in the 1960s, Thompson says; it's still floating
down a river of racial divide. When the Jena Six came along, they
poked everyone in the eye. A light was shined. He hopes Jena's
critics shine as much light on their towns as they shine on his. God
knows this little town didn't want the light. No town would. Will
they see the way forward or is their shame too great?

Reverend Moran doubts most people are ready to see anything. Not yet. He tells his Sunday congregation, I have seen
a lot of storms, but no storm lasts forever. There is something
better in front of us all, amen. Change will come by the hand
of our enemies—do I have a witness? They set off some things,
those noose-hangers. Sure did. To say they didn't know—well,
they know now, amen.

Susan Ory Powers lives near First Street among Jena's better-off,
including some middle-class black families, in a neighborhood
known as Snob Hill. In fact, the modest two-story brick homes
on the hill stand just one floor higher than the low ranch-style
houses a few blocks away. I see nothing particularly ostenta-
tious about them.

We sit at the dining room table for a dinner of rice and black beans and steamed asparagus. Her refined peppermint drawl, rising and falling with each enunciated vowel and consonant, suits the manner in which she presents herself: slight and trim, sun-colored hair, wearing a yellow blouse. Her grandfather was a mayor here in the 1920s; her uncle, a school superintendent. Her father owned a chicken farm and her mother handled loan closings. When Susan Ory Powers was a child attending grammar school, she and her mother drove past an American Indian girl. *If you're anything but nice to that little girl,* her mother warned, *you'll be punished. You behave. No matter their color.*

"That is the Jena I know," Powers tells me.

She was raised by black women—hired nannies whose children are now nurses' aides or cashiers. They live in Ward 10. It is much better now than it was then, she says. Nice homes coming up, not shacks. The people there have progressed. Not as much as she would expect of her own children, but considering where their families started out, enough.

After fourteen years in Los Angeles working as a set designer ("Every southern woman knows how to set a table, so I went to USC and became a set decorator"), she returned to Jena and the white, box-shaped house she had grown up in. Just weeks later, the nooses appeared in the high school's tree.

"What's this about?" she had asked friends.

In Los Angeles, she sought out black people because they understood her southern accent. A black man was a groomsman at her son's San Francisco wedding. He's family. If he wanted to marry her daughter, Powers would have no qualms other than that her daughter would have to get divorced first. That won't happen, she trusts, and therefore is left with the comfort of her convictions. She would not wish divorce on anyone.

She recalls the 1960s when the term "colored" was replaced by "black." In Jena, white people asked, What difference does it make? We've always called them "colored." It's part of our culture. What part of our culture are we allowed to keep without being accused of bigotry? "Hard to understand a word would make any difference then, isn't it?" She poses the questions rhetorically.

"More wine?"

A drizzly morning, first day of rabbit season. Haze Harrison hefts thirteen beagles, one after another, into cages on the back of his pickup. It's sunrise in Ward 10, and he's going hunting. Whatever rabbits he kills, he'll give to old folks. As the son of a sharecropper, he grew up eating wild meat because his family could afford little else. Long ago he lost his taste for it.

His one-story ranch-style house sits on a wooded street lined with warped trailer homes black-streaked from rainwater, their backyards wet as marshes. The asphalt street buckles into long stretches of dirt and gravel. Ward 10 might have improved from the days when people called it the quarters, but Harrison says it still ain't nothing to write home about.

Since 1970, Harrison has made Ward 10 his home. His front windows have looked out on burning crosses since then. For seventeen years he worked as the only black person among seventy-five white employees. He heard the word "nigger" at least three times a day, but Harrison won't work a job where most of the employees are black. No benefits. Just a lot of hard work and low pay. And most black people don't have money to hire anyone.

"Suzie, Sunshine," he calls to the remaining dogs dodging his outstretched hands.

He disagreed with the attempted-murder charge for what he considers a schoolyard fight, but he won't excuse the Jena Six for beating up that white boy. Kids aren't raised now like he was. He doesn't understand the younger generation of black people. He counts his dogs. These days, kids kill dogs if they get out of their pens and run loose. When he was a child, if it wasn't yours you didn't touch it.

"Spot, Shorty! Hush up!"

At Dewey W. Wills preserve, about a half-hour drive from his house, Harrison parks on a mud road made gooey from rain and lets the eager dogs out of their cages. He listens to them howl and take off after something, rabbit or deer he doesn't know, and follows eagerly, sinking into soggy ground.

As a black man, Harrison can go anywhere in Jena these days, eat anywhere, work anywhere—at least in theory. But blacks and whites still don't mingle. There are no white faces in Ward 10, except for a few spouses from mixed marriages. The town has grown subtler in its expression of its likes and dislikes. They don't just come out and say "nigger," but Harrison believes they think it. If a child grows up with that kind of talk, by the time he turns thirteen he's too far gone to think differently. Harrison doesn't know why that is. It's just what he has concluded about kids. Not all white teenagers. Some. That's enough.

"Hup! Hup!" Harrison calls to the dogs.

He heard about the tree long before it became national news. Black kids told him nooses were routinely left in a high school tree like it was nothing. He understood what was going on. It's not like it's anything new.

Harrison does not hate. His mother was religious. Not him, although he considers himself God-fearing. His older sister was killed by her husband. Harrison's mother raised his sister's children like her own and taught them to love their father despite his crime. Harrison visited with him when he was released from prison. Just the way Harrison was taught. Forgive the sinner. His stride picks up, propelling him through the woods after his dogs.

Hate destroys you, he says.

When teacher's aide Bobbi Cornett tells strangers she lives in Jena, she sees in their faces the hard look of distaste. *You're one of those noose-hangers*, they're thinking, and she knows it. The unspoken accusation burns. She's half Mexican. The charge of racism is way off, she tells me. She feels misunderstood, abused. On the day of the big September demonstration, Cornett woke up to the sound of helicopters, busloads of people, police everywhere. It was as if she had awakened in Iraq. Yes, that's it. She says that the demonstrators were misled about Jena, just like the country was misled about Iraq.

Cornett has lived in Jena with her husband and two children since 1980. Her father was an oilman, and as a child she roamed the world. Europe, the Middle East, Africa. Setting up house in Jena, she wondered, *Where the hell did we move?* At the supermarket she was unable to find fresh parsley and bottles of wine, only beer. It took sixteen years before Jena no longer considered her an outsider. Now she stands up for her town.

The marchers are socially conscious, she'll give them that. But terribly naïve. Cornett knows the mother of one of the noose-hangers, a special education teacher who ministers to the homeless and attends church. Cornett had even helped some of the Jena Six boys. What she has been told: the nooses were a prank. The boys didn't understand how a noose would be perceived. They weren't born in the time of Jim Crow. They had no notion. Who knows what kids are thinking? They aren't talking now. Can you blame them?

She had no problem with the attempted-murder charge. Knock a boy down, keep hitting him in the head, what would you call it? A schoolyard fight? She doesn't think so.

"Was there not violence implied in the noose?" I ask. She waves the question away. She's not a lawyer and won't comment further on the attempted-murder charge. That's for attorneys to decide, not the public.

"The Jena Six should be punished according to our laws," she says.

Her husband wanted to leave town the day of the September demonstration, but Cornett refused. No one was pushing her out of her house. I'm planting my flower bed as I planned, she told him. If the demonstrations turned violent, she would shutter the house.

In fact, she says, the demonstrators were very considerate and stayed off everyone's lawn. But they left Jena divided. This mess has plunged race relations back fifty years. She shakes her head.

"I'm half Mexican," she tells me again. "Why is this happening to us?"

When white people called Cleveland Riser "nigger," he mocked them. You don't have the education to pronounce "Negro," he told them. Your parents didn't teach you that. Their words didn't hurt Riser. He knows that a lack of intelligence causes fools to say "nigger," and he can get along ignoring them.

Riser is a retired assistant superintendent of schools. His defense is an educated mind. He dismisses racists by joking: They may hate him, but they still have to pay the taxes that support his well-earned Social Security checks. He just loves those people to death. "The money is not black or white," he says, and chuckles, covering his mouth to be polite.

He chose education over the plow and mule of his forebears, but his father and grandfather taught him the value of hard work and the self-esteem that comes with success. His grandfather grew the best crops, just outside Jena in Winnfield. Riser's father worked in the salt mines, but he emphasized education second only to religion. School buses didn't serve the black neighborhood they lived in, so every day he drove his son to the house of an elderly couple who lived along the bus route. He offered rides to fourteen other children too. He asked the school district for help with gas money but was turned down. Instead, black families paid him half a ham, potatoes, a quarter a day, anything they could afford to get their kids to school. All but two of the fourteen children attended college. Now Riser sees his education—the skills of the mind—as the best kind of empowerment, even against those who hate him for those skills.

Without skills, derogatory words cast a pall. Black people get tired of getting hit in the head with "nigger." The Jena Six, he believes, reacted in a physical way because they didn't have the words, the right words, to fight back with their tongues and intellects.

Some people have not accepted the fact of all these ethnic groups in Jena, Riser tells me. You find this in any town. It exists wherever there are barriers. Riser pauses, collecting his thoughts, the right words. You find this anywhere, he says. New York,

Chicago, Los Angeles. Anywhere. Jena's not so different in that respect. Barriers can be overcome, but conversation is better than battery. Words, used correctly, help to dispel fear. And fear, he says, still overpowers the residents of Jena. If your boss hates black people and you're dependent upon him, what words do you use? Do you use any? I work for him, I attend his church. I keep my mouth shut when blacks are discussed. I say I don't like them either to please him. I stop thinking for myself.

Riser was pleased to see all those people descend on Jena for the big fall protest. They brought an awakening to Jena. Good. Now some white supremacists plan to protest on Martin Luther King's birthday. Good, Riser says. Let them come. Black folks should react by not showing up. Think of it. No audience. Don't go, don't listen. Nothing would happen except that the hate would be ignored like so much wasted breath, wasted words.

The two little Dupre boys, not yet teenagers, dress like their daddy and granddaddy—army fatigues and black lace-up boots. They know how to handle a gun though they don't carry one holstered on their hips like the older men do. "It's going to come down to another Civil War," their granddaddy David Dupre Sr. says, and strokes his white beard. "I might not live to see it, but these boys will."

The boys look at him and then away, feeling awkward to suddenly be the center of attention. They play with a gray Chihuahua near a wall of mounted guns: .22 Magnum, .243 Remington, Winchester Model 94, Benjamin air rifle. Their mother works as a bank teller. This Saturday, the boys are alone with the men. "We have plenty of artillery. More in the attic," their daddy says.

"Ain't going to be between North and South, but between black and white," Granddaddy continues. "Blacks make it a race issue. I got kinfolk way back in history hung with a noose. It's a form of saying, If you screw up, you get punished. It's got nothing to do with blacks."

He pauses, asks me if I'm all right. Am I sure I don't want to hang my jacket? Am I sure I don't want some coffee? Bathroom just down the hall if I need it. Something seductive in his hospitality. Gentle, so disconnected from his rage. You seem like a good fella, Granddaddy Dupre tells me. "But if you're not, if you're some white liberal aligned with the Black Panthers . . . well, just because you got by me coming in, doesn't mean you'll get by me going out. Do you understand that?" The threat is expressed in such a quiet way that it doesn't quite register. I don't fully comprehend the fury beneath his soft tone of voice.

"Obama. Someone will kill him," Granddaddy says of the senator's presidential bid. "We'll have Obama Day. Ain't time for a black president. That nigger wins, I'll pack my shit and go to Mexico."

"I ain't that extreme, like they should go back to Africa, or anything like that," his son says. "I just don't like them."

He glances at his boys. Makes sure they're listening and understand.

Setting: Two seventeen-year-old boys, one black and one white, lounge on steps leading into the Jena courthouse on an overcast afternoon, waiting for a mutual friend who is inside appealing a speeding ticket.

> White kid: There's nothing to do here but go out of
> town. Ride around, watch ESPN.

Black kid: I'm trying to go to college. When I get my income tax refund, I'm leaving.

White kid: No future here. This mess with the high school, it's so big it's become my only memory of Jena. I don't want to say I'm from Jena anymore.

Black kid: The nooses made black people further mad than they already are. What did that mean? They'd hang us for speaking the truth? I feel like whooping some ass.

White kid: I'm leaving. But you know those boys made some money. My momma's boss is a black man. He said he saw one of the Six walking out of the mall in Monroe, hands full of bags.

Black kid: My manager at McDonald's—he's white, he's nice. Most people aren't racist. When I'm not at work, I stay in the house. I remember as a little kid selling blackberries in the white community. I was eight years old. Someone broke into a house somewhere around us. The police picked us up.

White kid: The way this has been handled, more mistakes are going to be made. My momma says I should go to New Orleans.

Black kid: Yeah, start over in a place where everyone's starting over.

There is no band. People silently carry placards:

> Dr. King said hate cannot drive out hate.
> Keep the dream alive.
> Black Power in Jena.
> It's a new day.

Down Oak Street, cars follow the marchers. Their arms are linked; others throw candy to children on the sidewalk. Without music, the march assumes the funereal quiet of news footage from another era. Ignore the wrinkles and gray hair, and a moment of youthful 1960s activism seems to stand resurrected.

The opposition, carrying *No to MLK* signs, seems equally lost in time. Some of them stomp back and forth in army fatigues. *Do we want the values of Jena or the values of a Detroit crack house?* Handguns holstered on their hips, living caricatures of white rage. Some walk dogs with nooses instead of leashes, demanding rights for the "white majority."

Half a dozen rotund members of the "New Black Panther Party," outfitted in black lace-up boots, black military uniforms, black berets, and Ray-Ban sunglasses, stand apart and refuse to speak with white people. They pick fights with police and shout triumphantly when one of them is handcuffed and dragged away, caricatures of a dated militancy that Jena's black youth are too young to recall. And then I see Susan Ory Powers holding hands with a black woman, and Bobbi Cornett in a van with black kids. I'm relieved by this, but their presence here isn't enough, any more than mine is. We seek absolution, but we are not absolved.

"I tell you what, Jena became the perfect storm of racial incidents," Reverend Thompson told me. "Yes sir, it became the perfect stage for America to play out its racial drama."

On a wet Tuesday morning, I check out of my motel and join the small procession of cars on Oak Street. Our headlights sweep past the vacant parking lots of Champlin's Furniture, Sonic, and McDonald's. The Martin Luther King birthday parade and the white rally that followed it left no trail of disruption. This new week brings a sense of relief that there will be no more commotion. For the time being at least, Jena will be quiet.

Dollar General, AutoZone, Popeye's. My headlights sweep the side streets and dark houses, as if to pinpoint a sleeping unease, the discomfort of distorted dreams, of something amiss. If it can be found, whatever *it* is, perhaps it will dissipate, be absorbed without interruption, or at least forgotten, in the days, weeks, months, and years that compose a life grounded in routine and unhindered by doubt. Or perhaps the marches will keep coming, the people will continue to talk, to try to understand, to forgive.

Minutes outside Jena, I merge onto Louisiana State Highway 127 and then onto U.S. 165; hours later I reach Interstate 530 and U.S. 71, and on and on, each household between Jena and my Kansas City home entwined in a loop of my own making, pulled together by our uncertainty and our yearning, each one of us an outsider in a collective search for common ground.

Smoke Signals

Dina McKenna
I'm so nervous Jill, Billy's cancer is now in the brain.
Five tumors which require radiation. You experienced
the same with your husband?

Jill Wilkins
Yes, Glioblastoma brain tumor.

FACEBOOK (October 21, 2010)

Strange to think about it, the black smoke.

As it turns out, the eventual killer of Billy McKenna was lurking in the photographs he snapped in Iraq. Billy wrote captions beneath some of his photographs; "Typical day on patrol" reads one. The photo is partially obscured by the blurred image of a soldier's upraised hand. Brown desert unfurls away from a vehicle toward an empty horizon, and a wavering sky scorched white hovers above. Off to one side: Balad Air Base and the spreading umbrella of rising dank smoke from a burn pit.

Billy told his wife, Dina, in emails from Iraq that the stench was killing him. The air so dirty it rained mud. He didn't call them burn pits. She can't recall what he called them. He didn't mean *killing* him literally. Just that the overwhelming odor was god-awful and tearing up his sinuses. Dina doesn't know when she first heard the words "burn pit." A Veterans Affairs doctor may have said it. The doctors were telling her a lot of things when Billy was on a ventilator. All she could think was, *How can he have cancer? He's indestructible. He's been to hell and back. He can build houses, race cars, fish, camp. He was an Eagle Scout as a kid. He doesn't smoke cigarettes.*

But Billy had been exposed to something much more harmful than cigarettes. Since 2003, defense contractors have used burn pits at a majority of U.S. military bases in Iraq and Afghanistan as a method of destroying military waste. The pits incinerate discarded human body parts, plastics, hazardous medical material, lithium batteries, tires, hydraulic fluids, and vehicles. Jet fuel keeps pits burning twenty-four hours a day seven days a week. The U.S. government, however, has only recently acknowledged the harmful effects of burn pits. According to a 2010 report by the Government Accountability Office, "burn pits help base commanders manage waste, but also produce smoke and harmful emissions that military and other health professionals believe may result in acute and chronic health effects to those exposed."

The Veterans Administration states on its own web page that chemicals, paint, medical and human waste, metals, aluminum, unexploded ordnance, munitions, and petroleum products, among other toxic waste, are destroyed in burn pits. Possible side effects, the department notes, "may affect the skin, eyes, respiration, kidneys, liver, nervous system, cardiovascular system, reproductive system, peripheral nervous system, and gastrointestinal tract."

The burn pit at Balad consumed about 250 tons of waste a

day, exposing 25,000 U.S. military personnel and thousands of contractors to toxic fumes. The pit was shut down in 2009, but the damage had been done. "Patients don't fully understand the implication of their symptoms," says Anthony Szema, the head of the Allergy Diagnostic Unit at Stony Brook University Medical Center, who has studied the effects of burn pits on returning veterans. "Most general internists don't know how to treat this. Hundreds of people are coming back [from Iraq and Afghanistan]. We have to create special centers of excellence within the VA with expertise to address this. We have to invent new drugs. Test sand, burn pits, what soldiers have been exposed to. Screen those exposed. We're talking a large-scale effort.

"The system," Szema added, "is going to be overwhelmed."

Of course the smoke would be harmful, Dina thinks now. But at the time of her husband's return from Iraq, why would she have thought anything about black smoke rising from something called a burn pit? What should a big hole in the ground the military used to destroy waste have meant to them? Why would she have thought about anything other than that her husband was home alive? Not that long ago Dina felt the wild, heart-thudding joy of her husband's return, the smiling-until-it-hurts kind of delight, that impassioned feet-off-the-ground body-crushing embrace of *I'm home*, but it seems long ago today without him here.

Dina and others have joined in the lawsuits against Kellogg Brown & Root, Inc., a Texas- based government contractor and its former parent company, Halliburton, alleging that it exposed American soldiers in Iraq and Afghanistan to lethal air pollutants by burning toxic waste. The heavy black burn-pit smoke lingered for days and even weeks at a time over U.S. bases and areas nearby, affecting soldiers and local populations. Claims against KBR and Halliburton have been filed in sixteen states by almost two hundred plaintiffs. The problem runs deeper than just KBR and Halliburton, however. The burn pits were intended to clean up Iraq and Afghanistan, to remove inevitable litter and detritus from the war zone. But in the process of cleaning up, the toxic smoke has become an unintended killer of American troops abroad. Of course Dina would much rather have her husband walk through the front door of the house than win a lawsuit.

Dina had been scared to death when Billy received his directive: *Your presence is requested . . . you are hereby ordered to report . . .* When a soldier was killed, everyone in both their families called her. How's Billy? Have you heard from Billy? She watched CNN nonstop. Looked for a familiar army patch, a glimpse of his face, anything to know he was okay. And he was, until he came home.

Nearly nine months after Billy died, on a muggy Florida day in May, when the cool of the morning has been consumed by the wet-plastic-wrap of afternoon humidity, Dina trudges from room to room, boxes in hand, and begins the tedious task of packing up her Spring Hill house. She and her two daughters will return to Long Island, where she grew up and met Billy more than twenty years ago, when he played bass guitar and dreamed of being a rock star. Dina will get the girls enrolled in new schools, and then what? She is forty-one and doesn't have a college degree. Maybe she'll work at a supermarket or become a receptionist. What does she want to be? She had wanted to be an army wife and look after her kids. Now, she must start over and find something else she wants.

An hour-and-a-half drive north in Eustis, Florida, Jill Wilkins sits in her study reading the latest entries on the Facebook Burn Pit page she set up after her husband, Kevin Wilkins, died of a brain tumor in 2008. After Kevin's death, the Facebook page was an outlet for her grief and anger. It gave her a mission: help veterans exposed to burn pits, and advise their families how to get the benefits due them. The page has become a kind of "chat" way station garnering more than nineteen hundred "fans." Jill dispenses advice based on her experiences with doctors, the VA, and her own loss.

Do you know what life insurance you have? she writes to one veteran who complains of ill health resulting from his exposure to burn pits. *Do you know where your paperwork is?* Jill had not known where her paperwork was when Kevin died. A lieutenant colonel in Kevin's Air Force Reserve unit made some calls on her behalf, so she had received his Reserve retirement benefits. Another soldier told her she was eligible for Kevin's VA benefits, which would help pay for her two children's school and health care. She was furious that she had found out by chance. Shouldn't someone have told her?

She wasn't worried when Kevin was deployed to Iraq. He was a nurse; he wouldn't be going to the front lines. She had grown accustomed to him being away once a month for his Reserve drills. His unit had been activated for the first Gulf War in 1990. She was pregnant. Back then she worried. But that time, his unit wasn't deployed. When the second Gulf War started and Kevin was called up, her children were teenagers. I can handle this now, she thought. Oh, she told friends and colleagues as casually as she might comment on the weather, my husband is in Iraq. She was proud of him, boastful. Jill never had a bad feeling about Iraq. She never thought Kevin would die.

Dina McKenna
I got a paper yesterday saying [the VA] will not accept service connection for the cancer but granted [Billy] unemployability insurance comp. I was also turned down for aid and attendance. I am very disappointed and so exhausted from the wait time.

Jill Wilkins
I don't care what their paper says. Never take "no" for an answer. And I also will do whatever it takes to help you guys. (I'm sorry, I'm just angry because more guys are dying!)

FACEBOOK (May 9, 2010)

Like so many others on Jill's Burn Pit page, Dina McKenna just appeared one day, another desperate spouse of a critically ill veteran. But Dina made an impression, perhaps because her last name was also the name of Jill's daughter McKenna. Dina wrote to Jill sometime in April 2010. Billy had been diagnosed with cancer and Dina had quit her job to take care of him. They had no money. Were they eligible for VA benefits?

Jill read the note again. Billy was dying. Just like Kevin. Once more, Jill's mind returned to the crowded hall of Florida

Hospital Waterman in Eustis, where Kevin worked as a nurse. He was on a gurney. A doctor was explaining the results of Kevin's CAT scan.

We found a mass.

What's a mass? Jill thought.

Kevin listened quietly. The doctor pulled up a chair and cautioned them not to get excited. Oh my God.

The doctor didn't know what the mass meant. Possibly an infection. Had Kevin been exposed to anything toxic?

Yes, Kevin said. To all kinds of stuff in Iraq. He mentioned the burn pit on Balad Air Base, where he worked in a clinic.

"Kevin said, 'I walked through toxic smoke every day,'" recalls Jill's friend Lori Ross, who was with Jill at the hospital. "He talked about the smoke and what was in the burn pit. He mentioned medical waste. It was more than just garbage. He talked about how thick and heavy the smoke was. He said it saturated the base."

Jill waited for the doctor to say he knew someone with the same kind of mass who had turned out to be fine. Instead, the doctor said he wanted Kevin to be examined by a brain surgeon at Florida Hospital South in Orlando. He told Jill to go home and sleep. Otherwise she would sit in the hospital all night. Okay, she said. She had two kids at home who knew only that their father had not been feeling well the night before.

The doctor left to arrange for an ambulance to transport Kevin to Orlando. Kevin asked Jill to buy him a chocolate milk shake at a nearby Steak 'n Shake. When she returned, she saw the doctor pacing back and forth outside Kevin's room tapping his chin, a worried look on his face.

Jill tried to make light of her own worry by teasing Kevin

about riding in an ambulance. Do you think it will have its lights on?

No, hon, I don't think so.

See you tomorrow. I'm going home to bed.

Might as well. I'll be laying around.

You don't have to tell me what to do.

She called Kevin later. What time will you get there? He didn't know. Don't worry, they'll have a room for me. See you in the morning, hon.

After she hung up, Jill played Monday-morning quarterback with herself. Why hadn't she realized something was wrong, seriously wrong? Kevin had been complaining of headaches for months. He'd say, God my head, and take Tylenol or Advil. Why would she have thought to say, Go get a CAT scan? He was the nurse, not her. They were just headaches, right? Everyone gets them.

Kevin had been tired when he left on his first tour of Iraq in May 2006. Had that made him more susceptible to the toxins he inhaled? Jill remembers him telling her, We all have cancer cells. When we get weak, they can get ahold of healthy cells and start to grow. However, at the time Kevin's focus was not on himself but on how Jill and the kids would do in his absence. When I'm gone, I don't want anything to go wrong, he said. I'll figure it out, Jill told him. I put an extra five hundred bucks in our checking account just in case, he said. Just in case what? Jill asked. You think I can't handle this?

Kevin would call her from Balad Air Base. What's going on? How're the kids? He told her he swam laps in an Olympic-size swimming pool once used by Saddam Hussein. The weather was very hot. There were two places to eat on the base, and one of them was not good at all. At night, insurgents fired mortars and he would crawl under his bed. He talked about working cases, taking care of kids. He never mentioned burn pits. By the end of his tour, in August 2006, he couldn't wait to return home. He celebrated by buying a Honda motorcycle and a 2007 Keystone Outback camper. They used the camper only twice before he died.

The headaches started around February 2007. A little nagging pain. The pollen was bad then, and maybe Kevin was allergic to orange blossoms. His eyes looked funny, like he had the flu. Something wrong, Kevin? Yeah, I'm really tired. What's for dinner?

Kevin returned to the Gulf in January 2008 and was stationed in Qatar with a medical air-transport team. He didn't mention his headaches when he called home. He wasn't the kind of guy who would waste what little time he was allowed on the phone talking about headaches. But the headaches continued when he returned home in April. At work, he wore a jacket and complained of being cold despite the Florida heat. Do you have the flu? his supervisor asked him. No, boss, I'm okay. He had sinus problems and was constantly blowing his nose. He had always received the best work evaluations, but he had become neglectful. He would forget to hang antibiotics, chart patients. His colleagues thought he was readjusting to being home.

Almost a year later, on March 25, 2008, he spent the night in the bathroom sick to his stomach. He was late for work the next morning. His supervisor told him he had kept a patient waiting. Are you okay? He told her he had been awake throughout the night vomiting. Go to a doctor, his supervisor said. The doctor referred him to the Waterman emergency room. He returned home to pick up Jill so she could be with him. She drove. He vomited twice out of the truck. In the ER waiting room, Kevin leaned his head back against the wall and closed his eyes. You all right? Jill asked him. Yeah, I'm all right. Jill bought a sandwich, came back, and looked at her husband.

They had met years earlier at a TGI Friday's restaurant in Orlando, where Jill worked as a travel director. Kevin was a friend of her brother-in-law. Kevin was the opposite of Jill. She was outgoing, he was shy. He lived in Kentucky at the time, but offered to delay his departure home so they could hang out for a week. This is it, Jill thought. They married in 1989, lived in Kentucky for five years, and then moved to Eustis.

Someone called Kevin's name, interrupting Jill's thoughts. An attendant led them into an examination room, and a doctor entered soon after. Kevin told him about being sick to his stomach. He mentioned that his head had been hurting for months. The doctor arranged for a CAT scan.

> Dina McKenna
> *Hey Jill, I took a few days off from the stress and now I am getting ready to fight back. Where do I start? I want to reapply for the service connected VA decision. Do I have to go to a VA rep for that?*

> Jill Wilkins
> *Dina, I will send you everything you need to. I am glad to see you took a few days off. You can make an appointment with your local VA rep then tell them why you are needing to file your claim. If you at all*

feel like they are giving you the "cold" shoulder (it hap-
pened to me) tell them you will come in and get the
paperwork that you need to file your claim.

FACEBOOK (May 14, 2010)

Dina closes Billy's book of Iraq photos and puts them in a box in the garage beside other boxes packed for the move to Long Island. It will be good to leave all the horror of Billy's cancer behind. For months, this house was nothing but illness. She has yet to remove the framed photos of Billy from the wall. Of him in his military fatigues, shaved head shining beneath the sun, holding their eldest daughter, Katie, in Colorado. It was snowing. Katie smiles, sitting on his knees. Of him in his twenties playing bass guitar, his shoulder-length hair waving about his face. Of him mowing the yard. He hardly ever cut the grass, so when he did, Dina snapped a photo. That was a fun day. A fun Sunday when all they did was laugh and enjoy one another's company.

Dina will leave the pictures on the living room wall for now. The house would feel anonymous without them. She has moved a few times without Billy, but not like this. Not with him gone, as in gone for good. She has all his stuff: six guitars, a toolbox, shoes, T-shirts. She can't sell them, doesn't want to. A stupid garlic press that was his too. Dina put it in his toolbox. She didn't know what it was. Maybe it was something he used when he worked on his car. Oh God, he laughed at that. Really laughed. A hissing laugh. He laughed the same way when he watched *Married with Children* and *Everybody Loves Raymond*. A very contagious laugh. Dina smiles. Frickin' garlic press. She doesn't know where it is now. Stupid thing.

She shakes her head and breathes deeply. Her daughters, six-year-old Sabrina and thirteen-year-old Katie, will be home soon from school. Billy always did homework with the girls. Dina worries Katie or Sabrina will come home with math and science problems she won't understand. She hopes Katie can help Sabrina with those kinds of questions. Katie handles math on her own, knows her mother doesn't understand it.

Dina surveys the refrigerator, thinking about dinner. Something simple. Steak. Billy was the cook. Fresh garlic, fresh basil. He had his own special recipe for everything. Dina looks at the ingredients in a cookbook and wonders, *What is all this crap?* Billy rarely bothered with a cookbook.

Okay, dinner. What else? Katie has a horseback riding lesson later. Dina might drop Sabrina at her sister's house nearby. Depends. Maybe Sabrina will want to watch Katie ride. Sabrina has been doing okay these past couple of weeks in school. No more time-outs. She had not understood Billy's death, and teachers telling her they were sorry. She began telling other kids she wished they would die. She didn't mean it. "Die" to her meant "go away."

Dina had Billy's photograph embossed on necklaces shaped like military dog tags and gave one to each of the girls on Valentine's Day two months after he died. Katie wears her necklace every day. Sabrina wore hers only once. Dina thinks kids at school asked her about it and their questions made her cry. Sabrina said she lost the necklace in her bedroom.

Sabrina is too young to remember her father when he was healthy. She only knew the sick Billy. He had begun having problems before she was born. After his first tour, he had complained about his breathing. He couldn't run without shortness of breath. Army doctors reminded him that he had grown up on Long Island; now he was based in Colorado. Altitude adjustment, that's all.

They called him "the old man from New York." He *was* old too, thirty-three when he joined. Before then he had been living the rock star wannabe dream. Gigs, drinking, staying up until 4 a.m. September 11 changed all that. He told Dina he would join the army. You do and I'll marry you, she told him. They'd known each other since high school, when she drove him away from a beer-drinking party the police had busted. He had the beer, she had the car. They were eighteen.

Billy and Dina married on New Year's Eve 2002. About four weeks later they left Long Island and took off cross-country to Billy's first duty station, Fort Carson, Colorado. Colorado was so different. Mountains and streams. Snow in frickin' April, man. Dina looked at the mountains and felt they were staring back at her. *Whoa*, she thought.

Dina and Billy had done it, escaped New York. Everybody else they knew had stayed behind, stayed the same. Not them. It was just the two of them, without the crowd. About a year after they moved, he was shipped out to Iraq.

Dina McKenna
Hello Jill, Bill's cancer relapsed, it's now in his nervous system, he has lost sight in one eye and half his face is paralyzed. I have been at the hospital every day all day trying to comfort him. The chemo is three times stronger now and every two weeks. I have been

contacting his former comrades asking for informa-
tion about what exactly happened over there. The
VA denied the claim of this being military related. I
appealed and am waiting for a response.

FACEBOOK (July 18, 2010)

Pastor Doug Edwards of Trinity Evangelical Free Church in
Eustis has known Jill Wilkins since 1995, when she and Kevin
first began attending his services. Jill called him when Kevin
was admitted to Florida Hospital South. Pastor Edwards had
his own doctor's appointment in Orlando. He visited with
Kevin and told him he would be fine. He ate lunch with Jill
and the children while Kevin had an MRI.

The MRI confirmed the existence of the brain tumor. The
next day, a Friday, doctors operated to remove it. Before the
operation, Kevin and Jill's son, Keaton, drew a heart on his
father's shaved head. No one had any bad feelings. The family
spent the day in the hospital waiting for the operation to be
completed. Kevin would get through this, Pastor Edwards
thought. They found the tumor and will remove it. This is a
slam dunk.

After the operation, the doctors let Jill and the children see
Kevin. He was sitting up, his head wrapped in a white bandage.
He was alert, but his speech was slurred from the anesthesia.
He wanted to take a shower. He tried to walk, but felt sick. He
complained that his head was hurting.

On Sunday, while talking to his mother, Kevin collapsed.
Jill was driving to the hospital when his mother called on a
cell phone. We almost lost him, she said. When Jill arrived,

she saw a chaplain outside Kevin's room. Kevin's surgeon ran past. What happened? Jill heard him ask a nurse. He was fine yesterday. The surgeon was shaking.

Jill can't recall how much time passed before the doctor came out of the intensive care unit to speak with her. Fluid buildup had put pressure on Kevin's brain, he explained, resulting in cardiac arrest. Kevin was on a ventilator. We've been checking on him, the doctor continued. There's no brain activity. He's not going to make it.

Jill called her pastor. How do I explain this to the kids? Jill asked him in a shaking voice. I can't. Your dad's on a ventilator? I can't. We did what they told us to do and now he's not going to make it? You have to be with me.

At the hospital, Pastor Edwards sat with Jill and her children. He spoke quietly, directly. He explained that Kevin was breathing with the help of a machine and would not survive. McKenna's eyes opened wide. She clung to her mother. Keaton stared at the floor. Neither spoke. Jill tried to remain calm but her voice shook, her face drawn and mournful. We don't know why these things happen, Pastor Edwards said.

He stayed with the family when the doctors took Kevin off the ventilator the next day. McKenna touched her father's face. Keaton held his hand. They watched a monitor show his heartbeat slowing to a stop. Everyone grieves in his own way, the pastor remembers telling Keaton. Military families lose their husband or father each time they're called up. Like a death, in a way. Gone but then they come back. Except when they don't.

Kevin had served on the church board. He was fifty-one, a down-to-business sort of guy. A get-it-done mentality. Very quiet, calm, in control. Three years after he died, Pastor

Edwards still feels sometimes that Kevin is on a deployment and will be back any day.

Why Kevin? Why a husband and a father? He has no answers. He didn't the day Kevin died, and he doesn't today.

Why Kevin? Why anyone?

Edwards shakes his head. He takes comfort in his belief that those who believe in God will have eternal life, but he doesn't suggest that this means Kevin's death makes sense.

> Dina McKenna
> *Good morning, Jill, Yesterday a VA rep was talking with me on the phone and said that my claim was denied because it's not "presumptual" that lymphoma is a part of the Gulf War. I told him I have living proof that it is and he told me I would have to change the laws and take it to the White House. I told him Exactly!!*

FACEBOOK (October 14, 2010)

Late one night, shortly before he entered the hospice, Billy stumbled and fell in the house. Dina screamed and closed Katie's bedroom door so she wouldn't see her father's agony. He looked like he was having a seizure but he was actually shivering against the tile floor.

Now, nearly half a year later, Katie and Sabrina McKenna burst through the front door of their house and veer off their separate ways—Katie to a breakfast-nook table where she picks up one of the family's three cats and sits beneath the hand smudge left on the wall where her father tried to break his fall. Sabrina scoots into the kitchen for a snack.

Hi, Dina says to Sabrina. Did you get a smiley face at school today?

Yeah.

What are you doing?

Washing strawberries.

You going to clean your mess?

Sabrina resembles Billy, same blue eyes and red hair. She likes it when people say, You look like your daddy. Dina thinks Sabrina resents Katie for having memories of their father. Like how they built model cars together. Seven in all, painted different colors. Katie has them in a box in her bedroom. Billy liked the purple car best. Sometimes she takes them out and looks at them arranged on the white knitted blanket he used in the hospice and that now covers her bed. His army cap hangs from the night table. Sometimes she wears it. Billy wore it when they fished together in Colorado. They would get up early in the morning while it was still dark and drive into the Rocky Mountains. She used worms, he preferred black spinnerbait. She would catch more fish than he did.

Katie, how was your day?

Boring.

Boring?

In archery I almost got a bull's-eye.

That's not boring.

Katie shrugs. She has long hair like her mother and wears jeans and a Carrie Underwood T-shirt. She held it together when Billy was sick, and did what needed doing. Okay, okay, how do I fix it? Katie said. Like it was her burden. Her fault. Her problem. It's not up to you, Dina said.

Katie made her father get-well cards and watched his favorite television shows and told him what happened. One time in the car, Dina tried to explain how ill Billy was. I know, Katie said, and turned up the radio. She didn't want to hear it. She was Daddy's little girl. She only broke down when Dina told her that her father had died.

Billy had been stationed on Balad Air Base his first tour. He spent some time in Baghdad too. He told Dina stories. How insurgents stuffed dynamite into the bellies of donkeys. When the animal exploded in a crowded market, guts and fur blasted everywhere. Billy would guard dead Iraqis while the army waited for their families to claim the bodies. He had to shoot the dogs that tried to eat the corpses. He also had to shoot at a boy who ran at some U.S. tanks yelling, Mister! Mister! Mister! The boy was told to stop but continued running. Billy never knew if his bullet killed him.

When he called home, he talked about the stink hovering over the base and asked Dina to send him Tic Tacs, sweet taffy, any kind of candy to get the foul lingering taste out of his mouth. He especially liked Jelly Bellies and always reminded Dina not to substitute store-brand jelly beans. It became a joke in his family, how particular he was about his Jelly Bellies. Dina stuck some of the candy in the pockets of the leather jacket she buried him in.

What are you doing? Sabrina asks Dina.

Waiting for the French fries. Do you want me to cut you some steak?

Can I have an Oreo?

No. Here, I'm cutting you meat.

I want an Oreo.

How about tomatoes?

All I want is an Oreo.

You can have two Oreos. But you have to eat your dinner first. Now do you want greens or celery?

Celery.

Deal.

Billy was home eleven months before he was called up a second time. Although he complained of being tired, he was okay. Still Bill. Drank beer on weekends, fished, worked on his car. Dina knew he would go to Iraq again. Soldiers were doing as many as three tours. It was a sad day when he showed her the deployment letter. He couldn't even tell her, simply handed her the paper. Dina just went on. She had Katie to look after.

Billy was afraid this time. He wasn't with guys he had trained with. His commander was a kid fresh out of West Point, and Billy didn't trust him. He told Dina he no longer understood why he was in Iraq. When he returned, he was diagnosed with traumatic brain injury and post-traumatic stress disorder. He received 80 percent disability from the VA and vocational rehabilitation funding. He quit the army and no longer wanted to remain in Colorado. His friends were leaving for war, but he was no longer a soldier. He wanted to put Iraq behind him. He enrolled at the Florida Institute of Technology in Orlando to learn how to build high-performance engines and rebuild classic cars, his passion since he was a teenager.

In Florida, Billy developed a lump on his jaw the size of a pencil eraser, and he began gaining weight. His face swelled. A doctor told him the lump might be from something he'd eaten and referred him to a dentist. The dentist found nothing wrong with his teeth and gums and suggested he consult a jaw surgeon. He was put on a waiting list. Three months later, the jaw surgeon found nothing wrong.

On Christmas Day 2009, Billy became short of breath when he and Dina took an evening walk. He sat down and thumped his chest, struggling for air. What's wrong? Dina asked him. I just need a minute, Billy said. They returned home and he went to bed. Three days later, he had trouble breathing again. Dina drove him to James A. Haley Veterans' Hospital in Tampa. As they entered the building, Billy collapsed onto a gurney. Hospital staff rushed him into the emergency room. After an hour, doctors told Dina that Billy had suffered complete kidney failure. They also found a mass the size of a pancake wrapped around his heart and lungs. The doctors didn't know if he would make it through the night. You're crazy, Dina thought. You got the wrong guy. He's only forty. You're not talking about Billy. Hospital staff kept coming to her with forms to sign. We need this, we need that. Do it, she said. Fix it. Do it.

Billy was on a ventilator for nine days. He fought when he was taken off it, tried to pull the tubes out of his arms, and was put in restraints. He thought the nurses were against him. He pleaded with Dina to untie him, sneak him some clothes. When she refused, he became furious. Get her out of here! he shouted. She's not here for me. The next day, he didn't remember it. The next day it was, Hi, babe, how you doing?

In January 2010, test results from the mass showed that Billy had T-cell lymphoma, a rare and aggressive cancer.

"Mr. McKenna has a diagnosis of lymphoblastic lymphoma," his physician, Donald C. Doll, wrote to the VA in May 2010. *"Mr. McKenna was exposed to multiple chemicals and toxins by the burn pits while serving in Iraq. Exposure to chemicals and*

toxins have been linked to the development of lymphoma. This exposure to chemicals and toxins while in the military in Iraq is a causative factor in Mr. McKenna's lymphoma. Sincerely, Donald C. Doll, MD."

What did Daddy tell you about Iraq? Dina asks her daughters as she gives them their dinner. Share your memories.

Not much. Got really hot, Katie says.

Do you remember him talking about the rain?

No.

All the rain would be black because the air was so dirty. What do you remember about Daddy, Sabrina?

He'd throw me in the air in a pool.

I know he shared jelly beans with you. He hid them under his bed. I was rotating the beds after Daddy went to heaven and found a few under there. How many times did he take you to Walmart and not tell me what you bought? He'd come back and say, Oh we didn't buy anything.

He bought three lures one time, Katie says.

Billy wasn't released from the hospital until February 2010. Months and months of driving back and forth, one hundred miles a day between their Spring Hill home and the Tampa hospital, ensued as Billy received chemotherapy treatments. But the doctors held out little hope. They tried radiation to prevent the cancer from spreading to Billy's brain, but the rest of his body was falling apart from chemotherapy. It was a year of medical information Dina didn't want to know. Just fix him, she thought. She had to give permission for the doctors to use powerful doses of chemotherapy. Just show me where to sign, she said. What was she supposed to say, No, use a weaker kind?

On July 16, 2010, a doctor wrote in Billy's chart, "Patient is currently limited to his hospital room. It is unlikely he will improve due to the nature of his illness." Billy's doctors advised against further treatment. Go home, enjoy the life you have left, one doctor told Billy. No, I want another treatment, Billy said. Start it right now. I want it now.

Phil, Billy's best friend from New York, moved into the house to help care for him. Billy no longer wanted Dina or the kids with him. He didn't want them to see what he had become. He was six feet two, and by the time he died, he weighed just ninety pounds. Dina and Phil kept him as comfortable as they could. Billy listened to the TV, Phil babbled on about songs and movies. Billy's dad drove down on Christmas Eve from New York to see him. Billy told his father, I'm going to die. With Dina it was, If I don't make it, do this. Instead of breaking down, he got angry at her. Shouted, threw things. Everything she did, it seemed, was wrong.

One night he told her who to give his guitars and fishing tackle to when he died. And he made her promise that Katie would only marry someone who could identify at least fifteen different tools. That was as close as Billy came to saying goodbye.

The night he died in a hospice, Billy's father roused Dina from a couch. It's time, he said. You need to wake up. A nurse was checking Billy's pulse. Dina crawled into bed with him. She pressed close against his body. The nurse looked at her watch.

Time of death, 10:50 p.m., she said.

Dina McKenna
My husband passed away on Dec 28 from a cancer

*caused by burn pits . . . I just found out that 2 other sol-
diers from his unit had/have scar tissue on their lungs.*

FACEBOOK (January 12, 2011)

Sometimes Keaton Wilkins thinks, I won't ever be able to go camping with Dad again. Or he'll see a movie and think, *Dad would have liked this.* His father was a fan of the *Fast and the Furious* movies. He was going to give Keaton his motorcycle; I'll get a new one and you can have the old one. It was a piece of his father he wanted, but his mother hadn't known that and gave the bike back to the dealer when Kevin died. It was an honest mistake, but a piece of his father was gone.

The biggest deal about his father's death was that it happened so fast. He was going to be better and then he died. Just like that. Keaton and McKenna were home when their mother called from the hospital. She told them not to go to school. They needed to come to the hospital. She would not say why. Keaton knew she was upset. He heard her strained voice as she held back and tried to remain in control. A neighbor drove Keaton and McKenna to Orlando. Neither one spoke.

Keaton's memory begins to turn cloudy at this point. He stares at his lap. Maybe he does not want to remember. He struggles, pulling reluctantly at details that give him pause, the words cracking as he speaks while he tries not to cry. He and McKenna went into some kind of room, like a conference room or something. Their mother was sitting down, her face drawn, pale. Pastor Edwards was there. Keaton's mother told them their father was in a coma and then broke down. McKenna began crying too, and Keaton held his mother. He felt a weird kind of suspension that left him unable to feel before her words rushed in on him again and he struggled to breathe.

Afterward, he went in to see his father. All the tubes inside him. Then he went outside and took a long walk, thinking, *I'm going to lose my dad.* Thinking, *Maybe he'll get through it. Because yesterday the doctor said everything was going good.* Thinking, *The doctors have given my father twenty-four hours. If there's no brain activity, he's not coming out of it. This will not end well.* Then trying not to think.

He remembers crying alone in the hall on one of his walks. He remembers Pastor Edwards talking and then remembers embracing his mother when she said she had agreed to remove life support. He remembers the warmth from his father's hand slowly fading when his heart stopped.

Keaton is sure his father would not be angry with the military. He just would have thought it should have done a better job protecting the troops. Keaton only heard his father cuss once, when he had trouble backing the camper into a campsite. He was not a complainer.

One day, a normal day, Keaton was playing video games when he heard a slight noise from his mother's bedroom. She was crying. McKenna was with her. She called Keaton over and held onto him and said, I miss your dad so much. Keaton sat on the bed. Why aren't you crying with us? his mother asked him. He stood up. Mom, Keaton said, we all deal with this in our own way.

His family, Keaton says, is usually drama-averse. Something comes up, they tend not to exaggerate the problem or make a big show of how to get through it. Stay calm, that's their attitude. Some days are better than others. Like his father, Keaton doesn't complain.

The morning after Billy died, Sabrina had a school field trip, Katie a riding lesson. Dina let them have their day. She told them when they got home. Katie cried. Sabrina fidgeted, confused by the grief around her.

Dina spoke with the VA in the following days. My husband just passed, what do I do? I need to get him to New York and buried where he grew up. Don't you escort the body? Won't his unit carry him from the hearse to the cemetery? His death was war-related. Don't you take care of that? She was told to get a death certificate and submit it. Billy stayed in the morgue for six weeks until she received his death certificate and mailed it to the VA. Eight weeks later, she received $2,000 for burial expenses.

Billy was buried in Calverton National Cemetery in Suffolk County, Long Island. A plot for Dina is beside his. He did not receive a military escort from Florida to Long Island. His unit did not attend the funeral. The funeral director and his staff carried the coffin from the morgue to the hearse. Cemetery maintenance men carried the coffin from the hearse to the grave. The coffin was draped with a flag.

You excited about moving to New York?
    Yes, Sabrina says.
    What's the best thing about it?
    Snow.
    You saw snow before.
    When?
    The last time we were in New York.
    When was that?
    Sabrina looks away.

Daddy's funeral. You forgot the word or don't like to say it.

Forgot it, Sabrina says, still staring at the floor.

Dina continues cooking. She has so much to decide before the move, but the empty house is confusing without Billy. She has no one to share decisions with, and is afraid of making bad ones. Like what to do with Billy's car? She's keeping it. Just like his guitars, his T-shirts, and that frickin' garlic press, if she ever finds it. But how to get the car to New York?

What are these? Katie asks.

Folders. Put your schoolwork in them. You have a hole puncher?

No.

I'll get you one.

Billy put everything into his car, a 1972 Plymouth Duster, an old stock car he bought in Colorado. It didn't run but the body was perfect. He had been slowly restoring it, a piece here, a piece there. Brakes, electrical work. Hood scoop. A 440 engine, 750 horsepower. He did all the math in his head. This part goes with that. He never used a manual.

When he got sick, he continued ordering parts even though he knew he didn't have time left to install them. They were all but broke. Dina was struggling to buy milk, and there was Billy ordering fenders. He'd have them delivered to a friend and then his friend would sneak the parts into the garage. He planned to paint the car flat black, no shine. He died before he could do that, but he lived long enough to hear the engine. Oh God, did he hear it. The carburetor was so fierce, gas shot up to the ceiling through the open hood. Billy had an audience of about twelve friends, and they all started applauding. He was as excited about the car as Dina had been giving birth—when the baby came out and Dina went, Holy shit, a baby. That was Billy's response to his car starting for the first time.

A triumphant November afternoon. I built that, I built that, Billy said. Earlier in the month, the VA had found in favor of Billy's appeal for service-related benefits: *"As evidence of record confirms that you served in Iraq, we have conceded that you were exposed to environmental hazards, specifically multiple chemicals and toxins by the burn pits as discussed in the opinion of Dr. Doll."*

The next month, Billy died.

> Dina McKenna
> *Jill, I got a phone call this morning from a VFW rep and he said a decision was made on Friday that Bill is 100 percent totally disabled. The cancer is service connected. I should receive the papers in the mail soon along with a retro check from back in January when I originally filed the claim.*

> Jill Wilkins
> *Dina, please copy and paste your above note to me on my burn pit page for all to see. We need more positive comments on my page and you can inspire more people to keep trying.*

FACEBOOK (November 1, 2010)

What do you have again? Jill writes to an Iraq war veteran who has contacted her on the Burn Pit page. She has not heard from him in months but he assumes she remembers him. She can't even remember to send her children to the doctor with the right insurance card, let alone all these followers. She must focus on things other than advocating for families of burn-pit victims, Jill reminds herself. Like paying for her kids' college. Keaton is a college sophomore; her youngest, McKenna, about to graduate high school. They still need her, as they do their father. But Jill is the one here.

Jill had many good years with Kevin. So good she could live off that joy for the rest of her life. Still, she doesn't want to become an eccentric old lady living alone with a bunch of stupid cats. She's only fifty-one, she says. It would be great to meet somebody. She could see it happening and at the same time not see it.

Can she ever replace Kevin? Never. At night she says a prayer thanking him for watching the kids. Or seeks his advice when something breaks. Kevin's colleagues at Florida Waterman Hospital tell Jill they have "Kevin moments." They walk past his picture in the hall of his workstation and pause. Or they see a patient in a military uniform and are reminded of Kevin's service. Or one of them brings in food. Kevin was always right there for food. Give him a McDonald's sandwich and he was so happy. Patients continue to ask for him. They assume he has been redeployed.

One day on Balad Air Base, Kevin tended an injured Iraqi girl. She would not sleep unless he held her hand. When he let go, she woke up. So he held her hand and didn't let go. Jill imagines him glancing around the clinic, glasses perched on his nose, wondering, *What am I going to do next?* Chitchatting with the other nurses, a nonchalant smile on his face. The girl asleep, his hand closed around hers.

Sometimes Jill wonders if Kevin knew what he was walking through when the burn-pit fumes washed over him. If he knew the smoke was toxic. What would he have done if someone had told him, You will walk through a toxic smoke cloud every morning to do your job? Would Kevin have said, Well, I'm not going to do that? Would he have chosen duty over family? Kevin was a good soldier. If that meant he had to go through foul-smelling smoke, he would do it. Even if he thought it was not a smart idea. He did what he was told.

Dina McKenna
Sabrina's Kindergarten graduation tonight . . . she wishes her dad was here . . . I gotta hold back the tears . . . Big fat ice cream cones after the ceremony!!!

Jill Wilkins
Those special times are always going to be a little hard . . . always have friends and family members with you, it helps a lot!

FACEBOOK (May 26, 2011)

After dinner Dina reminds Katie to get ready for her riding lesson at Hart Horse Farm. Dina calls the stable, surrounded by dense trees and the buzzing chatter of cicadas, her quiet place. Birds and bugs, Dina says, are good for the soul. She steps out into the garage and waits for her girls, runs a hand over the Duster, fingers lingering. Before he died, Billy and Dina had talked about hitting the road. When he got off treatment, got off the chemo, they'd go. Why not? Homeschool the girls. Fish in every lake. Screw the world.

Let's go, Dina calls to her daughters. Billy saw Katie ride one time. He was too weak to get out of the car. He wore a patch over one eye and watched her out the passenger window. She wasn't a little girl on a pony, he said. She was a girl controlling a horse. He cried. He made Dina promise to buy her a horse when she turned sixteen.

Dina smiles wistfully. Sometimes, when she reads posts on the Burn Pit page, she thinks, Stop the fight. Enjoy the time you have left. But Billy couldn't stop fighting. She doesn't really expect anyone else to, either. Nor should they. She hasn't.

She thinks of the photograph Billy took in Iraq with the smoke from the burn pit fouling the horizon. Strange to think about it, that black smoke. That it was as much an enemy as the insurgents. Maybe more so. How it took the life of her husband, leaving her and the girls behind. How it took Jill's husband too. A father just like Billy. Strange to think so much time has passed and still she and Jill struggle to move out from under its shadow.

Dina hopes to meet Jill and thank her for her help, advice, and support. Someday. Not now. Not yet. Dina needs to sort her life out first. She doesn't want to just burst out crying when they get together. Instead, when the time is right, she'll stand before Jill and show how, with Jill's help and her own resolve, she pulled her life together again. Dina imagines they will talk for hours. She will tell Jill how Billy comes to her when she least expects him. Like the other day, when she cooked ravioli. She had never made it before. She just knew. Billy, she believes, guided her. Another time, she poured his mouthwash out into their bathroom sink. When she walked back into the bedroom, she smelled him. That menthol fragrance on his breath.

I made a card, Sabrina says, walking into the garage. She holds a folded piece of brown paper sprinkled with glitter and presents it to her mother.

For me? Dina says.

Yes, read it.

I love you.

Cool. What's it say inside?

Read it.

Thank you for everything.

I accidentally spilled glitter, Sabrina says.

On your bed?

On the cover of my thing.

What thing?

Just a thing I made it on.

Well, it's a beautiful card. Very nice and thoughtful of you.

Thank you for everything, Dina reads again. She smiles, wipes tears from her eyes.

May I ride my bike?

Sure. Sabrina.

Yes?

It's going to be all right.

Maybe.

Definitely.

We Are Not Just Refugees

The sad-looking man with the forced smile works the counter at Church's Chicken. He takes orders and sweats in the numbing glare of heat lamps. His dark, lined face strains. He has an engineering degree from Kabul University. He was an interpreter for the U.S. Army in Afghanistan. At thirty-one, he knows he should not be working here.

"Spicy or regular chicken, sir?" he asks a customer in a monotone, weary from repeating the same question over and over again.

"What?"

"Spicy or regular, sir?"

"Spicy."

His coworkers call him Sam, a crude shorthand of his Afghan name. He prefers it that way. *Have you known fear?* he asked them when he was hired. *If some bad people back home know where I am, no matter how slim the likelihood of that, the family I left behind will be in danger. Do you know that kind of fear, sir?* Of course they do not. The less they know about him the better.

"Drink, sir?"

"A regular Pepsi."

"Would you like a side with your order, sir?"

"What?"

"A side, sir?"

"Fries."

Sam works 11 a.m. to 5 p.m., five days a week, for $700 a month. He wipes tables, mops floors, serves food. Between customers, he wrings his fingers in frustration.

"I can't make out your accent? Where're you from?" the customer asks.

"Kabul City, sir."

"What?"

"Afghanistan, sir."

"Damn. Hey, give me one regular and one large drink."

Sam looks for a girl to pour the sodas. The kitchen ovens roast him.

"Get the spicy strips!" his manager yells.

Sam retrieves them, the desperation of his servitude cutting through his eagerness to please.

Sam arrived in the United States in January 2008 on a special immigrant visa created specifically for those Iraqi and Afghan nationals whose lives have been threatened because of their work for U.S. forces. The Iraqi translators, drivers, and assistants of all sorts face near-certain death at the hands of one militia or another. Hundreds of interpreters serving troops in Iraq and Afghanistan have been killed, targeted by militias, assassins, and kidnappers. Causes of death ranged from booby traps to evisceration. Hundreds more have been seriously wounded. Many lost limbs. Some lost their eyesight.

The special visa allows translators and their immediate families to gain admission to the United States, apply for permanent residency, and eventually acquire U.S. citizenship without jumping through the innumerable hoops that other refugees must. However, applicants face a series of different hurdles. They must be a citizen of Iraq or Afghanistan and have worked directly with the U.S. Armed Forces as a translator for at least twelve months, obtained a favorable recommendation from a general or flag officer, and cleared a background check and the required screening.

If approved, still another set of challenges awaits them. Refugees without special status are automatically referred by the U.S. government to a social service agency before their arrival for assistance with housing, employment, English-language classes, and other needs. Refugees with a special immigration visa, however, have no government liaison and must rely on contacts they made among their American employers in Iraq or Afghanistan for help once they arrive in the States. Otherwise, they could easily be left stranded at the airport, essentially homeless.

Once here, refugees need to earn a living. Many had professional careers. They were doctors, lawyers, engineers, and university professors, among other professions, prestigious in their own countries. Here, however, their credentials often don't meet U.S. standards. They won't resume their careers until they learn English and study their professions anew in American universities. Their expectations confront a humbling reality: they must take whatever job they can find, no matter how menial.

Sam lives with another Afghan interpreter, thirty-one-year-old Ahmadi, in a spare, two-story house in east Kansas City. It is owned by Janet Dean, a single woman who, until she met Sam, had lived alone for nearly thirty years. He was walking with his wife and son on a January afternoon and saw Mother Dean, as he now calls her, kneeling in dirt, planting flowers. He waved and she waved back. He asked her, Madam, do you know of a park where I can take my son? From his accent, it was obvious he was not American. She took a long look at him and heard God tell her he had a need.

Sam told her that for the past three months he had been living with an Army veteran who had befriended him at Bagram Air Base, a former Soviet military installation occupied by American troops outside Kabul. He and his friend stayed in the cold basement of a one-bathroom house shared with eight other people. Mother Dean told Sam his family could move in with her. Instead of paying rent, he would help with the upkeep of the house. One morning later that month, he woke her up in a panic. *Mother!* he shouted, *my wife is very sick.* They drove to a hospital and she gave birth to a healthy baby girl. Six months later Ahmadi, Sam's neighbor from Kabul, moved in, along with his pregnant wife and two boys.

At sixty-one, Janet Dean, a short, stocky woman with large eyes that peer out from behind round glasses, was set in her ways when she offered her home to Sam. When she found cereal and marshmallow crackers on the floor from one end of the house to the other, she got irate. Ahmadi's children used to swat at her cats. *No hitting people or cats*, she told them in a no-nonsense voice with hints of taffy-toned southern drawl. The kids know how to say *good morning*, and that's about it. They now say *good morning* to her morning, noon, and night. In the evenings, she sits at her kitchen table and bounces Sam's baby girl on her lap. Sometimes it's good, sometimes it's irritating. She has her moments, but she reasons that life is one constant adjustment. Isn't it?

Sam and Ahmadi bicker like an old married couple. For instance, on this summer evening, Sam forgot to stop at a supermarket to pick up some bread after work, and Ahmadi scolds him when he walks into the house. Ahmadi arrived just ten days ago. He does not have a job or a car yet and resents his dependence on Sam and Mother Dean. In the morning he will stop by Jewish Vocational Service (JVS), a refugee resettlement agency in downtown Kansas City. His case manager there was an Iraqi interpreter for the U.S. Army in Mosul and goes by his army nickname of Bob. Bob has advised Ahmadi to move to Timberline, an apartment complex closer to his office and other social service agencies, but so far Ahmadi has refused. He wants to stay near Sam.

Sam also has an appointment with a caseworker. He hopes to attend a local university and get a degree, perhaps in business management, so he can find a better job. He does not want his children to see their father serving chicken. In Afghanistan, he lived in a tall, square, six-bedroom house with his mother, father, three brothers and their wives and children. They owned another house about fifteen miles outside Kabul. He had attended private schools where he learned English and engineering. He had recently graduated from Kabul University when New York and Washington, DC, were attacked on September 11. He and his family watched bombs fall on the outskirts of Kabul after a U.S.-led international military coalition attacked Afghanistan in October. It surprised him how quickly the Taliban had fled.

A neighbor working at Bagram told him they needed translators, and Sam began interpreting for the U.S. Army. He followed soldiers into caves in Helmand Province, a former Taliban stronghold. Afghanistan was not dangerous then, in the spring of 2002. But gradually, year after year, a resurgent Taliban emerged. Outside Kabul, suicide bombings, kidnappings, roadside bombs, and violent crime became a part of everyday life. The renewed violence killed an estimated eight thousand people last year, quadrupled the rate of insurgent attack, and frightened away many foreign investors. Increasingly, Afghans who worked with the Americans were called infidels and traitors. Sam sensed a bad future. U.S.-backed Afghan president Hamid Karzai had problems. Under the Taliban, northern people such as himself had been targets. Under Karzai, interpreters were now targeted. Sam stopped telling even his friends that he worked for the Americans. It was getting too dangerous to stay.

He can't begin to explain how difficult it was to leave Afghanistan. He had always lived in Kabul. He had never left his family for more than ten days. He was crying so hard when he drove his family to Kabul International Airport that he did not remember how he got there.

A Pakistani man he met at a Kansas City restaurant managed a Church's Chicken franchise and told him about a job opening. Sam began work the next day. At first he was instructed to clean tables with a rag. *What do you do?* his wife asked him when he returned home from his first day at work. He didn't answer. He cried for three, four hours. But he went back the next day.

Like Sam, Ahmadi had arrived on a special visa. He started looking for an apartment immediately after he settled in Mother Dean's house. He paid dozens of thirty-dollar application fees, only to be told by prospective landlords that he could not move in because he had no rental history, no credit, no job.

Why, he wondered, didn't they tell him this before they took his money? Finally one landlord offered him an apartment and Ahmadi gave him a deposit, but he needed more money to cover the first month's rent. Bob told him not to worry. He would receive a federal assistance check specifically for refugees. Ahmadi waited three or four days but the check never came. The landlord said he would not wait for him any longer and gave him back his deposit but kept the application fee.

Ahmadi had been an English teacher and an interpreter for international aid organizations in Afghanistan before he began working for the army. He read a flyer distributed by American soldiers in Kabul promoting jobs to English-speaking Afghans for $800 a month, much more than he had ever earned before. He recalls the arid mountain villages where he interpreted on behalf of sergeants, captains, lieutenants, generals. He met with powerful warlords. He would stay with the army for months and then go home. He thanks God he never saw combat. Never saw death.

He will never forget his house in Kabul. Seven rooms. Dozens of carpets on the floor. Visiting with friends like Sam. He wept when he said goodbye to his family. He chose Kansas City because Sam lived there. The people are very nice, but he feels strange, alone. Not too many Afghans here. The summer air is wet and sticks to him. He misses Afghanistan, despite its dry heat and dust and dirt and fighting. I love my tired country, he says. In Kansas City, he notices how clean everything is. Fragile. What can he touch without making it dirty? Neighbors don't visit neighbors as they do in Kabul. No one checks on anyone. When Mother Dean was sick with flu, no one came by to see her.

When Ahmadi taught English in Kabul, he enjoyed the look

in his students' eyes when they began to grasp the language. A sense of possibility emerged that was much bigger than words. When he interpreted for the army, he earned enough money that he did not charge his students. He would like to teach in Kansas City, but no university will accept his Afghan teaching credentials. He applied for a Social Security card so he could look for some other work. His application was lost, however, and he must reapply.

Ahmadi does not understand why he needs a Social Security card or a job other than teaching. A professional teaching certificate should be honored no matter what country issued it. But look at Sam, an engineer. He serves chicken. Ahmadi no longer trusts that the government will help him. He loved teaching, but maybe he too will clean tables.

An impossibly thin, stooped-shouldered man in sweatpants and a Bass Pro fishing T-shirt much too big for him, Ahmadi walks upstairs to his room for his laptop computer. He visits Islamicfinder.org ("Prayer Times for 6 Million Cities Worldwide") and listens to the voice of a mullah rise out of his speaker. He kneels on a bath towel and prays. Islam is a very nice religion, he tells the Americans he meets. The Taliban did not understand it. He was fortunate to avoid them, for the most part. When the Taliban governed, Ahmadi worked in the countryside teaching English to Afghan doctors employed by Western aid organizations. After six, seven months he would come into Kabul to visit his family. Then he would have problems. Taliban police suspected him of trimming his hair and beard, a violation of their interpretation of Islam. He was jailed. He told them they defamed Islam, and they beat him.

Sam waits for Ahmadi in the backyard. Jets of water burst from sprinklers hidden in neighboring yards, *hiss, hiss, hiss*ing as they rotate. Bugs buzz above his head, darting in and out of drifting cottonwood seeds. Sam listens to the soothing pulse of the water and lets his mind wander to escape the greasy odor of his clothes.

He cannot thank Mother Dean enough for her kindness, but he yearns for independence. Three cats. Dirty carpet. Small house. *How long,* he asks himself, *will we be housekeepers?* For how long will I clean here and at the restaurant? He translated for the U.S. Army. He met with ministers and generals. *We are not just refugees,* he says of Ahmadi and himself. *We are special.*

Sometimes he awakens in the night after dreams of his life in Kabul. He had good friends. On Friday nights they came over to his house and stayed into the early hours of the next morning. A friend called recently from a wedding party. *We're all together but for you,* he said. *You are not with us.*

Awake, Sam wants to make tea but instead stays in bed and waits until he hears Mother Dean stir. She works as an insurance adjuster. He does not know what that is but it requires her to get up early. He doesn't want to disturb her walking down the creaking stairs while she sleeps. Sometimes she gets angry and Sam thinks he has made a mistake. What has he done? Did he dirty the carpet? Did his son break something? No. It is not about him at all. She is angry about something else. Still, he stays in his room. Stays very quiet and worries.

Outside Kansas City, in suburban Gladstone, Bob, Ahmadi's caseworker at JVS, sits in front of his laptop, barefoot in T-shirt and shorts, and lets the time pass before he goes to bed. Framed certificates documenting his work with the army hang from his walls. *For exceptional service as an interpreter.* A copy of *The Ultimate Weight Solution: The 7 Keys to Weight Loss Freedom* by TV personality Dr. Phil McGraw gathers dust on an end table.

"I like Dr. Phil. He's a smart doctor," Bob says.

He checks out YouTube and listens to rock 'n' roll. He contemplates digital photos of his time with the army. "This guy was shot and sent to Germany," he says of an American soldier in sunglasses smiling for the camera beside a Humvee.

He doesn't know what to say about Ahmadi. Bob showed him a couple of apartments besides Timberline, but he didn't like them. They were too far from his mosque, too far from Sam. He'll need a job once he finds a place. Hotel, factory, restaurant work. Ahmadi wants more, but he needs to begin somewhere. Bob knows he was fortunate as a single twenty-seven-year-old refugee to settle in so quickly with a job that made good use of his education and experience.

Maybe he wants a five-star hotel or a mansion, a coworker had joked of Ahmadi. Bob didn't laugh. He understands the difficulty of adjusting to America. At first he was confused too: stunned, a little fearful, trying to take in all the different sights, odors, sounds. He didn't know anybody. In the three short months he has lived in Kansas City, Bob has learned to be very aware. There were no rules in Iraq. Here you have to be on time. Time is very important. He learned that in the army. You have to drive at a certain speed. You can't go fast. You have to look at people when you talk to them, even though in Iraq that would be considered disrespectful. Strangers ask him where he is from. *Iraq*, he tells them. They don't know what to say. *What religion are you?* they ask. *Muslim?* They think he's bad. A terrorist.

"This is a photo of soldiers giving candy to kids. They take, but they still hate us."

The insurgents had very good intelligence. One day another interpreter told Bob that his photo was found among captured insurgent documents. He was shocked. He didn't know how they got the 2004 picture of him partying with other interpreters in one of Saddam Hussein's many palaces. It didn't matter. He had to leave. With the recommendation of his commanding officer—*his ability to convey the intentions of Coalition Force patrols helps ensure the safety of the people of Mosul, and he wishes nothing more than to become a citizen of the U.S.*—Bob secured a special visa in three months and left Iraq in March 2008. He stayed with an American soldier he had worked with who told him about JVS. Staff there helped him find a one-bedroom apartment in Timberline. They hired him as a translator and caseworker for the increasing number of Iraqi, Middle Eastern, and Central Asian families coming to Kansas City.

Bob studied English in school. He had trouble with American slang, but those words were not part of the army's oral and written examination when he applied to be an interpreter in October 2004. He passed easily. They placed him with American combat units. Daily patrols. *How do you like it with Americans here?* he was instructed to ask Iraqis. They were very happy, they told him. U.S. soldiers were invited to lunch, dinner. They were given flowers. Then it started getting bad.

"Here we are at a university searching for munitions," he says of a photo of U.S. soldiers searching a room of overturned desks.

He wore a mask to conceal his identity. He looked in the mirror and thought he resembled a burn victim. *You want a nickname?* his commanding officer asked him. *To protect your identity?* Yes. *We'll call you Bob.* The mask sucked—a slang word he had picked up. Hot as hell. Sometimes when he was in a Stryker combat vehicle, he would take it off and throw it away. At night, when no one could see him, he didn't wear one. One time his patrol captured an Islamic man they thought might be terrorist leader Abu Musab al-Zarqawi and took him to a jail for questioning. Six months later he was with a different unit, and they stopped the same man. *Don't you remember me?* he asked Bob. *You arrested me before.* Despite the mask, the man had recognized Bob's voice.

Iraqis hated interpreters more than the Americans. Without interpreters, the Americans would be helpless. Like turtles without shells. Bob could see the hatred in the Iraqis' faces. When he visited his village home in Sinjar on leave, he told friends he had been abroad studying or that he had a job in another part of Iraq. Something like that. Whatever appropriate deceit popped into his head.

By the time he left Iraq, his patrols had been hit with twenty-five improvised explosive devices, two car bombs, and three suicide bombers. Heads here, arms over there, patrol after patrol. Snipers were the worst. You couldn't see them. They hid in the trunks of cars and shot at you through the rear lights. A soldier would just fall down. At first Bob thought the prostrate soldier was just dizzy from the heat, until he saw the blood seeping from his head.

"This day we found a huge weapons cache," he says of a photograph of guns, mines, and mortars.

One afternoon his patrol received word of a suspected suicide bomber. They shot a guy matching the description, then checked his ID. He was not the guy. Shot in the forehead.

He was sixty-something, an old man out shopping. Bags of fruit and bread were in his backseat. It surprises Bob not to hear gunfire in Gladstone. He enjoys living in a place without fighting. He likes the quiet. He will help Ahmadi appreciate his new country. Bob can't speak for Afghanistan, but in Iraq it was dirty all the time. Very dusty. Very hot. Very loud. He doesn't miss it like Sam and Ahmadi miss Kabul. He would like to bring his parents to Kansas City. He won't tell other Iraqis here that he worked for the army. They might be sympathetic to the insurgents and report him and threaten his family. It makes it difficult to have friends. When he sleeps he dreams of blood.

The following morning Sam drives with Ahmadi the thirty miles from Mother Dean's house to JVS. Long drives wear on his 1994 Dodge. It died shortly after his army friend gave it to him for $1,200. Sam spent $1,600 getting it repaired. In addition, he spends about $200 a month on gas and $550 a year for insurance. *I give you all I have*, he tells the car.

"I have no money," Ahmadi tells Bob when he enters his office. "You said I'd be getting a check."

"Let me see," Bob says.

"Shit," Ahmadi says.

Bob shuffles through some papers. Sam asks for his case-worker.

"I don't know where he is," a woman tells him.

"He said to meet him here today."

"So was he planning to talk to you today?"

"About three, four times we've scheduled meetings. This is not effective. I need a plan."

"Sure. Of course you do."

Sam looks at his watch. He has to be at work in twenty minutes and turns to leave but Bob calls him back.

"You are employable," he says, "and eligible for a six-month federal matching grant for refugees. Two hundred a month, and forty dollars each for your two children. Your wife gets seventy because she's unemployable."

He punches a calculator. "That's eighty-seven and a half dollars a week. Wait." He sorts through some forms and then consults with another caseworker. "Okay, there's no money for unemployable. Just you and two kids. Your wife's not eligible for this. Sorry."

"Shit."

Sam approaches another caseworker and asks about his appointment. "He will see you," the caseworker says, pointing to a chair. "He'll be here in a second. Sit."

"I have to go to work."

"Then come back. Forget your problems for now and enjoy the day."

Sam steps into a corner sliced with shadows. At this rate, he feels he will wipe tables and serve chicken forever. Families from Africa and Burma stand nearby and squint in the glare of the hot afternoon sun as they wait to be seen. Ahmadi walks over to Sam while Bob uses the phone to make an inquiry. They huddle together. *What are you going to do?* they ask each other. *I don't know, what are you going to do?* Sam looks at his watch, shakes Ahmadi's hand, and leaves for work.

"Okay, I just called Timberline," Bob tells Ahmadi. "They have an apartment but it won't be ready for two weeks."

"I can't wait. I want to rent near my friend."

Four seventy-one, please, sir, Sam tells a customer. *For here or to go, sir?*

"We know Timberline. They work with us. You don't have rent history. Other places, they just want to take your application fee and waste your time. That happened to me. We can't rent to you, sorry. But they have your money. Timberline is much better. I stayed two months at Timberline. It's close to here. They pick you up and take you where you have to go."

Do you want a side, sir?

"If I take it, how will I get appliances to cook?"

"They provide all that."

"Do I have to wait in an empty room until they provide it?"

"No."

Ten-piece, seven ninety-nine plus tax, sir. Here or to go?

"I don't want to wait."

"This is your fault. I showed you Timberline before, when they had an apartment, but you didn't want it."

"Is it safe and quiet?"

"Yes, but you didn't like it. I think you should take it. As soon as an apartment opens up we will get you the rent money. What are you going to do?"

Anything else, sir?

"Shit."

That evening, Ahmadi and Sam reclaim their spots in the backyard of Mother Dean's house. She organizes dinner in the kitchen with their wives. *Not a crumb on the floor*, she noticed when she came home. Sam's six-month-old baby lies asleep on the living room rug between fallen sofa pillows, undisturbed by the clatter of a washing machine. Ahmadi's toddler runs through the living room. A gray cat flees.

The smell of barbecue filters above the heads of Ahmadi and

Sam, hinting at the Fourth of July celebrations that will start on the weekend. Neither Sam nor Ahmadi quite knows what the holiday means for them yet. They have security with Mother Dean but not independence.

Sam will try to see his caseworker another time. Ahmadi has decided to move into Timberline, as Bob suggested. Sam will visit him, and when Ahmadi gets a car he will visit Sam. He would prefer to stay close to Sam, but Americans, he has come to understand, don't live with family or near their friends. He and his wife and children will remain with Mother Dean until he gets his check.

He considers the absurdity of his position. He can't rent an apartment because he doesn't have any money. He doesn't have any money because he doesn't have a job. He doesn't have a job because he doesn't have a Social Security card. He shakes his head. He had friends who came to America and then returned to Afghanistan. *Why did you come back?* he asked them. *Go and you will see*, they told him.

He and Sam cannot return to Kabul. Their work as interpreters puts them and their families at too much risk. Insurgents might consider them important enough to kill or kidnap. Others might consider them traitors. *You worked for the infidel people*, they would say.

If it were not for Sam and Mother Dean, it would be very hard for Ahmadi. He has no place at the moment other than her house, no friend other than Sam. He must live where he can find an apartment, work where he can find a job, even if it means wiping tables. It is not good or at all special, but for now, here in the United States, it is enough.

New Missions

Reynaldo "Rey" Leal, 28, Edinburg, Texas
Iraq deployments:
September 2004–April 2005
January 2006–July 2006

You remember the little shit more than the big shit.

Or maybe, Rey thinks as he puts a clothing bag and his camera in his car, you remember the big shit too, but in a different way. Certainly Fallujah was hell and deserved its own category of shit. Some days he thinks of Fallujah and the other bad shit when he served in the Third Battalion, Fifth Marine Corps Regiment. Days with too much unaccountable time. Days that were especially difficult after his discharge, when he lay awake in his Edinburg, Texas, home consumed by thoughts of Iraq.

These days, Rey has little time for distractions. He's married and enrolled in college and the father of a four-year-old son. Wife, son, school. Yet when the U.S. withdrew all its forces from Iraq in December 2011, the war came back to Rey big-time. It will live in his mind for the rest of his life, and despite all the yellow-ribbon car magnets and *Support Our Troops* bumper stickers, it seems to him that most of the country has allowed the war to fade from its consciousness. The war remains in Rey's dreams, and in the sorry stories he hears of returning soldiers trying to find space in a civilian world. Its end has made him wonder how marines in his unit are coping at home. Marines he hasn't seen since his 2008 discharge.

Pete Perez, Corpus Christi, Texas. Pete talked with a smile. Even when he was serious, it never took him long to get back into that smile.

Levi Simmons, Searcy, Arkansas. Hey, you hillbilly, marines would shout at him. I ain't no fucking hillbilly, Levi would drawl. He shot a pigeon one time. I don't give a fuck, he said. I killed this bird, I'm eating it. They were all sick of the ready-to-eat meals that plugged them up so badly they chewed tobacco to take a dump. Levi rubbed the pigeon with barbecue sauce and roasted it. Ate the fuck out of that pigeon. Tasted like hell. A staff sergeant said Levi'd get bird flu.

Kenny Fredenburg, Branson, Missouri. High school wrestling champ. Loyal. Tell him to run through a wall, he'd do it, no questions asked. A martial arts cage fighter now.

Kurt Poliska, Rochelle, Illinois. Nice guy. Considerate. Not a dick. Didn't need to throw his weight around to make a point. Some marines called him weak. If you're not a dick, they said, you can't lead marines.

Apolonio "Polo" Topete, Sioux Center, Iowa. What had he written on his helmet? "What's really hood, bitch?"

And Rey. He was ten years old when his father died. A boy who became the man of the house. As a marine he was a hard-ass. When he returned from his first deployment, after earning a Bronze Star in Fallujah, he was promoted from private first class to corporal. All of a sudden it was, Hey, you're a corporal. A higher rank than some of the guys who had commanded him only weeks before. Weird. He knew he had to prove himself. Be extra tough, extra motivated. He let nothing slide.

Pete, Levi, Kenny, Kurt, Polo. Rey was their team leader in his second deployment. Good marines, each one of them. What do they think about the end of the war? How are they doing?

To find out, Rey will use his college winter break to visit each one of them. Another mission. He contacted them on Facebook, and they sounded eager to see him. Recently, Kenny stopped responding to Rey's messages. Busy, that's all. Maybe he's in a tournament and just forgot to tell Rey.

Seeing the guys again will be strange at first. They'll probably keep saying, What's up? What's up? before figuring out where to begin. Some of them might be okay with their memories of Iraq, some not. Rey will joke that he just wants to update their portraits. They'll laugh. You were always taking pictures, they'll tell him.

In Iraq, everyone managed in their own way. Some guys sang, played guitar, played videos. Rey snapped photos. Looking for that one shot, that one piece of beauty amid the insanity. He would volunteer for patrols just to take photographs. The guys looked at him self-consciously at first, then they grew to like it. The photos gave them a piece of themselves back to themselves. I'm alive at this moment, in this frame. Look.

Rey had been into photography long before the war. As a kid in Texas, he would leave his trailer park home in Edinburg and spend his days in the air-conditioned public library looking at *Life*. He liked the contrasts of blurred images to distinct images in the magazine, and how even the blurred images made sense, and how some pictures looked better in black and white while others looked better in color. So he taught himself photography by snapping pictures of flowers and members of his family. By the time he joined the high school newspaper, he had a portfolio.

The first member of his family to complete high school, Rey also earned a college scholarship, but he wasn't in the mood to follow through with it. On television he watched the 2003 assault on Baghdad and decided that where he was, Ohio's Bowling Green State University, was not where he needed to be. He dropped out and enlisted in the Marine Corps. You can't do this, his mother told him. You feel too much for people.

Rey finishes packing the car, looks at the directions to Pete's house, his first stop. He leafs through other sheets with blue lines showing the routes he'll follow into Arkansas, Missouri, Illinois, and Iowa. There will be other marines he won't have time to visit. Like Mendez in Los Angeles and Hawley in Seattle. And there is one marine Rey cannot visit: radio operator Lance Corporal Geoffrey R. Cayer.

Soft-spoken kid, nice, but seen as meek. Did that push Cayer? Rey asks himself. That feeling of not being part of the family, the pack? The day Cayer died, July 13, 2006, Rey had just come in from a patrol. He walked into a room that held ready-to-eat meals and looked for a chemical light. He noticed Cayer staring at the ground off to his left. Cayer was about to go on guard duty.

What's up, Cayer?

Nothing, Corporal, Cayer said.

Rey left, slipped on his iPod, and slept. When he woke up four hours later, the sun was just starting to go down. He walked outside, put on his Kevlar. Someone, he can't remember who, told him Cayer had just been loaded onto a bird.

What do you mean?

He's dead.

What the fuck are you talking about?

Shot himself, Corporal.

The chaplain walked past. Rey didn't move. They only had one more week in-country. One fucking week left, and Cayer killed himself? What the hell? Ambushes, tank mines, snipers. They all knew the chances of dying. Fifty-fifty, Poliska liked to say. Rey just wanted to get everyone home alive. One week to go. It seemed Rey would not be asking those questions. Then Cayer died.

Rey doesn't understand what happened. Neither do some members of Cayer's family, who question whether it was a suicide at all. According to at least one report, a sergeant told the Cayer family that in the war zone where he was, his finger would have been on the trigger of his weapon constantly. An accidental discharge is a possibility, the sergeant said. Some of Cayer's friends think it was a freak accident. The military says it's still under investigation. Rey, however, has no doubt that Cayer killed himself.

What if I had asked him why he was looking at the floor if nothing was wrong? Rey thinks. Would Cayer be alive today?

Highway 77 twists and turns past quiet homes beneath a wide, dark Texas sky that only hints of morning with sun-streaked pale blue hues. It can still feel strange to Rey, cars passing so close to him, drivers with no cares in the world.

He remembers the morning he saw a battered semi swerve around traffic on the shoulder of the highway that marines had shut down for an IED sweep. He yelled Stop! and tossed a flare. The truck picked up speed. Another marine raised his M16 and lit up the truck's tires. It continued racing toward them. Another machine-gun blast lit up the grille. Water and steam spewed out. Rey raised his weapon and aimed at the driver. He saw his bearded face through his gunsight and was about to squeeze the trigger when the truck sputtered to a halt. The driver was just a dumbass in a hurry or some stupid shit.

Behavior like that made some marines hate the Iraqis, but not Rey. Why're you trying to learn their language? they'd ask him. Because we're here, he said. He thought Iraqis would appreciate him trying to speak to them. Might be a foot in the door.

On his second tour, he tried to look at things from both sides. Do this and this might happen. Do that and suffer those consequences. He would tell Simmons and Fredenburg: Understand that when we bust in somebody's door and assault their mother and father, it doesn't matter how justified we feel, they will hate us until the day we die. When we hit a house, it always has repercussions.

Other marines didn't care. Their attitude was, Fuck hajis, but Rey liked the culture; drinking tea, smoking tobacco from a hookah pipe. Some of the guys told Rey, Yeah, sure, they give you tea, but they might poison it or shoot you when you leave. Rey didn't think so. Some marines saw his trust as weakness, but Rey thought not seeing the other side of things was weakness.

Pete Perez, 27, Corpus Christi, Texas
Iraq deployments:
May 2003–December 2003
January 2006–August 2006

Pete tells Rey that Iraq was something he did and now it was done. The way he sees it, Saddam was a bad dude. That was enough for him.

Well, not completely, Pete concedes. Saddam being a bad dude and all did not excuse sending five-year-old children out of their homes in the middle of the night so marines could use the buildings as control bases. Told them, You need to leave for four days. You need to go to a cousin's house or some shit. Pete had little brothers and cousins. He has two children now. No, Pete had hated kicking kids out of their homes.

Baghdad reminded him of Mexico. Paved roads with dirt on either side. Concrete houses painted green and blue. His grandmother's house was concrete. Big highways, hotels. During his first deployment, before he knew Rey, Pete stayed in a palace basement. Plumbing broke, water all over the place. Floors above, Paul Bremer, who led the Coalition Provisional Authority, had an office.

Pete worked security at that time. Got a few attacks: rockets, small-arms fire. One time he heard a hiss right over his head, and then a wall exploded. When the smoke cleared, Pete saw nothing but rubble and a guy covered in dust running through a cloud.

Remember Post Alamo? he asks Rey.

In Zaidon, Rey says. Nothing but mud huts and broken roads.

One night some marines decided to eat a can of chicken with ramen noodles. Someone put the can on the fire without cracking the lid, and it exploded. Got hot chicken on one marine's face. The sergeant thought they were being mortared.

Pete joined the Marine Corps in 2002. He had graduated from high school but did not want to attend college. He didn't want to sit around on his ass, either. One November day at his uncle's house, as he considered brochures from different branches of the military, his uncle suggested he join the best, join the Marines.

It was a different time. His friends were like, You're joining the Marines? Oh good, awesome. Then, in about 2005, it changed. Yeah, around 2005 or 2006. People would say, You're in the Marines? Oh man, that sucks. I wouldn't do that. These days, every now and then someone might thank him for his service, show some gratitude, but not as many as before.

Rey, remember that first patrol we went on, and I shot that dog?

It was a big Cujo-like thing. It and two other dogs hauling ass, running toward Pete. He hoped they'd run by, but the first dog jumped him. Pete unloaded on that dog.

How about Staffos, remember him? He didn't know parts of an M16. What's this, Staffos? I don't know. C'mon, Staffos, Pete would tell him, this is your weapon!

What about Cayer? Rey says. Remember him?

Cayer was a little like Staffos. Kind of slow, Pete says. He'd always get an ass-chewing. But he couldn't have killed himself for that. He would have shot himself a lot sooner if he had been upset about ass-chewings.

It sucked being in Iraq, but you signed up for what you signed up for. Cayer knew that, Pete says.

We had one week to go, Rey says.

Pete doesn't dwell on the war. He's married, studying mechanical engineering in school, raising a family. He thought people would make it a bigger deal when the war was over, but they were like, Oh really? They don't know. They don't know how exhausting it was to kick kids out of their homes, set up security, go out on patrol, and three days later move to another house and kick out another family. The families were fucked. They would be seen as friendly to the marines, and their houses would be destroyed by insurgents as soon as the Americans left.

He thinks about that, not about Cayer. He tries not to think about any of it, but he does.

Highway 77 continues north, twisting through small towns boasting multiple Burger King and McDonald's restaurants. Rey turns off onto Highway 59 and drives through Houston and Lufkin and Longview and finally Texarkana, crossing into Arkansas.

Who would have imagined that he and Pete would survive Iraq, marry, have children, and enroll in college? Throwing families out of their homes really bothered Pete. Rey can still see a mother and father and two kids leaving their home and walking off in the dark. We're all going to hell easy, Rey thought. Everybody has that thing, one memory. Can't overplay the bad shit, can't underplay it. Can't say, That's nothing to what I saw. They all saw different things.

During the early months of his first deployment, it hadn't really hit Rey that he was in Iraq, in a war. He was based out-side the Iraqi city of Fallujah. Beautiful. Lakes, palm trees, little huts around the lake. A getaway for Saddam Hussein's son Uday. A lot of mosques. Square concrete buildings. Fallujah was much more developed than Rey had expected, but its peace would soon be shattered. In November 2004, the Third Battalion, Fifth Marines, entered the city to confront thousands of insurgents encamped there.

Rey held his breath for the first two blocks. He turned corners, saw bloated bodies. A head lodged beneath a taxi. Cats and dogs tearing through clothes and eating legs, arms, torsos.

Walking down streets just seeing it, rubble crunching under-foot. Going from house to house, three or four marines. Big iron doors they would blow open and then they'd rush into the building. Clear it room by room, house by house, block by block. All day, every day, through the end of December.

When they stopped for the night, the marines took turns on watch. Stay up one hour, two hours, then it was the next man's turn. They would have no idea who might be in a house two or three blocks down, so they set booby traps as a precaution. Broken glass under doors, on top of windows. Pots on top of closed windows. That worked too.

Some days nothing. Sometimes a stretch of nothing days. Other days, they would find houses filled with weapons. A wall of one school was stacked with mortars, artillery, AK-47 rifles. The marines kicked in a door to one place and found a group of Iraqi men huddled in a corner. No rifles. Sons of bitches had laid down their guns somewhere, the marines assumed, so they couldn't smoke them. Killing unarmed men would violate the rules of engagement. It kind of sucked that someone had to die before the rules of engagement loosened up. The leashes would come off for about a week, then it was back in your cage.

The marines were so pissed. Rey doesn't know what they might have done to the Iraqi men they found if a lieutenant had not been present. He won't say they would have lined them up and shot them, but they didn't even have that option. Not with a lieutenant there. They arrested them. Bastards. They were lucky that marines had found them and not the Iraqi army. The Iraqi army would have smoked them, lieutenant or no lieutenant.

Then there was that really old guy the marines found. He

was like someone who stays in their Florida home despite warnings of a Category 5 hurricane bearing down. This has been my home for fifty years, and I'm not leaving, no sir. Wearing pajamas. Marines clearing the street, and he pops up. Only reason they didn't kill him, he was ninety-something years old. A terp—interpreter—talked to him, let him know what was happening.

Rey can still smell the dead bodies. Bloated. He was not used to seeing a grown man's belly out to here. He thought that if he looked at them long enough they would pop.

Levi Simmons, 24, Searcy, Arkansas
Iraq deployments:
January 2006–July 2006
October 2007–May 2008

A framed photograph of Cayer stands on top of a shelf of DVDs in Levi's apartment. Glasses, cap, green fatigues. His narrow face expressionless. Levi found it in the battalion office at Camp Pendleton in a closet instead of hanging on the wall with everyone else who had been killed in action. Levi thought that was fucked up, so he took it.

Cayer. He always had that face, Levi says. Mad, happy, sad, he always looked like he was sucking on a lemon. Levi used to put rat traps in his bed. Cayer had the top bunk. Levi put the traps on every step and in the bed. Goddamnit, think you're funny, Cayer said. He would get into bed and set off more traps. He got back at Levi by nailing the door to his room shut. Levi laughs. Goofy as hell, that kid.

I'm glad I didn't see him after he shot himself, Rey says.

I saw him. I think about it, Levi says.

Cayer felt he couldn't talk to us.

We were dicks to him but meant no harm, Levi says.

I said to myself, This kid had problems, but he couldn't tell us. I feel that's fucked up.

I don't know. It still leaves another momma crying for her boy for no reason.

Levi pushes his shoulder-length hair out of his eyes. He pats his beer belly and tells Rey he needs to lose weight. He lives by himself. His wife left him during his second deployment. Took $20,000 of his money with her.

You don't do that to somebody, Levi says.

Also in his second deployment, Levi learned to smoke Valium and heroin from hookah pipes. When he inhaled heroin, he felt twenty feet tall. Exhale and it was like falling through a beanbag chair. He bought the drugs from Iraqi police. His sergeant got pissed—marines stoned, lying around not doing anything. When he got home, he had the shakes and threw up for days. You want to know about it, go there and find out, he tells anyone who asks him about the war. It took about a month for people to stop asking him how many Iraqis he had killed.

He stays in his apartment or at his mother's house. He doesn't like sitting by himself. Sometimes he spends time on the water, fishing. Catfish, crappie, bass.

Remember Zaidon? Levi says. There were no roads to some villages. I worried about old folks. I wondered if they knew a war was going on.

At Abu Ghraib you ran over a mine, Rey says.

Three times. It was that mud puddle.

The Humvee wasn't heavy enough to set it off.

I hit the pothole on purpose to fuck with the guys in the Humvee, Levi says. I didn't know there was a mine in it.

I remember your face when you found out. White.

At least it will shoot you straight up in the air, Levi says. One good thing about a mine.

Levi feels bad for the Third Battalion, Fifth Marines, deployed to Afghanistan. About twenty guys died in Sangin, Helmand Province, before the unit returned home in March 2011. Levi would have been there with them had he reenlisted, but what good would it do to add another body to the meat grinder? It would not have changed anything. You step where you step. Maybe on a cigarette butt, maybe on a mine. What's meant to be is meant to be. Who knows whether if Cayer had gone to college instead of Iraq it would have ended differently for him.

Levi shoves himself off a couch and grabs a beer from the kitchen. He never sleeps, he says. Gets up, showers, starts drinking beer. No hard stuff; he doesn't act right when he drinks hard stuff. Sits here and drinks thirty beers until he finally crashes. The VA wanted to pump him full of Ambien. They were like, Anything happen over there bothering you? A friend shot himself to death, how's that? Do you have PTSD? Want pills? They didn't understand any more than his momma does.

Downing his beer, Levi stands in his living room, uncertain what to do next. He wants to go out, but where. The VFW? A strip joint? He reaches for another beer. He doesn't know why he joined the Marine Corps. He didn't see a recruiter. He and his cousin had talked about joining, and then Levi just went and did it. A few days later he asked his mother, Can you give me a ride to Little Rock? Why? I need to go through the military enlistment process. It was all BS. He took a loyalty oath, piss test, physical. They made him squat and do a duck walk to see if his joints were flexible.

In-country, during his first deployment with Rey, Levi would ask, Do you think we'll get in a firefight today? He was eager. He was eighteen and a dumbass. The first time a bad guy shot at him, he was handing another marine sunflower seeds. *Zing!* Goes by his head. What the hell was that? Sounded like two two-by-fours slapped together.

Some of the places we slept, Rey says.

That one house. Nasty smell. One room was stacked with goat shit.

Cammies get so stiff they'd stand up.

Socks got nasty. Boots got nasty, Levi says. Supply guys said, No, we don't have anything to give you. They were wearing the new stuff. Assholes.

Levi frowns. He works on his beer, stares at the photo of Cayer.

Cayer told Levi that he was not supposed to be in Iraq with a deployed unit, but in the States. Everyone gave Cayer shit; getting on him was like a car salesman giving shit to the car washer. Cayer was nineteen, maybe twenty. Never drank. Levi didn't think he had been with a woman, either.

Minutes before Cayer shot himself, Levi had asked him for a cigarette. He hadn't taken more than a few steps when he heard the shot. What was that? What the fuck? Levi ran to Cayer. What do you do? Give mouth-to-mouth? Not with his brains hanging out of his mouth.

Cayer and everyone else got killed for what? Freedom, people tell Levi. Shit. Levi's free here. He didn't know why he was in Iraq. He understood his orders, understood what he had to do on any given day, but he didn't know why he was in Iraq. What's the big picture? Don't worry about it, other marines would tell him.

If he were to kill himself, he would not go out wearing heavy-ass Kevlar like Cayer. If that dumbass could do that to himself, what's to stop Levi from doing it to *himself?* Some guys weren't bothered by it at all—they saw suicide as a weakness, nothing more. It would have been different if Cayer had been killed by an IED or a sniper.

Don't worry about it.

Still, Levi does.

In the morning Rey leaves Searcy, turning onto Highway 65 for the three-and-a-half-hour drive to Branson. He enjoys the drive. The rise of the road over hills, deep tree-lined valleys below him. He still hasn't heard from Fredenburg. Once in Branson, he will look up Kenny's girlfriend on Facebook and see if he can track him down through her.

Levi's use of heroin troubles Rey. It showed inept leadership on the part of Levi's commanding officers. You are who you are because of who led you. No way would Rey have put up with that shit. He would have had Levi on patrol 24/7, so he would not have had time to smoke that shit.

Being aware, alert, was the only thing that kept him alive. Especially in Fallujah. Fallujah stayed twisted. The Americans had this Iraqi who would speak through a big intercom thing. Attention! Attention! he would say in Arabic. Drop your weapons! Then he would do this deep, evil laugh, *heh, heh, heh.* The PSYOPS guys played Metallica CDs full-volume to keep the bad guys awake. Kept the marines awake too.

The insurgents weren't stupid. Most were college-educated

and in their early twenties, as compared to the average eigh-
teen-year-old high-school-educated private. But sometimes
they did stupid things. They shot at a tank one time. Rey didn't
understand why they took on a tank. The tank swiveled around,
boom! Tank one, insurgents zero.

The marines got tired of getting shot at and pinned down.
They began prepping houses with artillery fire. Lit up those
houses for Rey doesn't know how long. Maybe two magazines'
worth. Sometimes they would fill water jugs with gasoline and
then add Styrofoam so it would stick to shit and wrap the con-
coction with a flash-bang, similar to a firecracker. Test it by
throwing it into a room, watch doors blow off their hinges. All
right, it works.

One time, they were told not to shoot people with a .50 caliber
machine gun. Technically, the weapon was meant only for vehicles. Shoot someone with .50 cal, all you had left was pink mist.

Kenny Fredenburg, 25, Branson, Missouri
Iraq deployment:
October 2007–May 2008

Twenty-four hours after he arrives in Branson, Rey is sitting in
a cramped cubicle in the visiting room of the Taney County
Jail beside Kenny's jujitsu instructor, New Jersey native Rick
Koenig. Together they face Kenny's image on a small video
screen and speak to him through telephone receivers. Kenny's face balloons and shrinks as he shifts in his seat. The light
catches the red-and-white stripes of his prison uniform, the tat-
toos up and down his arms.

Colors fit you well, dawg, Rick says. Can you see us?

Yeah.

See who's here with me?

Yeah. Hi, Rey.

Kenny has been incarcerated for seven days for failing to report to his parole officer. He had recently served a ninety-day stretch for drunk driving. Rick tells Rey that Kenny also has a prior history of assault and destruction of property, usually under the influence of alcohol.

Rey had met Rick the previous night at Botanas restaurant and bar, where Rick works as a bouncer. Small world. Rey recognized someone in the bar he had worked for in Edinburg. He mentioned he was looking for Kenny, and his former employer introduced him to Rick.

I got bad news, Rick told Rey. On December 26, Kenny had trained with Rick. They talked about him losing weight. Kenny smiled, a little embarrassed, and said, Yeah. That night he called Rick and said cops were at his door. What did you do, dawg? Nothing, Kenny said. But he was scared. Rick heard the police kick in his door, heard Kenny resist arrest.

What's it look like? Rey asks Kenny.

Going to court Tuesday.

What can we do for you?

I don't know. I got twenty-two probation fines.

Here's the deal, Rick says. I'm here for you.

Kenny had walked into Rick's gym about a year ago. He sucked. He needed to fill so many holes in his fight game, but dawg, he had heart. Kenny never questioned Rick. If Rick called him at 2 a.m. to train, Kenny was all in. He would run flights of stairs again and again. Three hundred and fifty-two steps. Four times in five minutes. Kenny listened. He did whatever he was told. Rick never asked him about Iraq. He knew enough without knowing. Kenny had demons, Rick said. Ray Charles could have seen that.

Get ahold of my mom on Facebook, Kenny tells Rey. She doesn't know where I am. Man, they kicked in my door. Said it looked like I didn't live there, and that gave them the right to kick it in. Came in with guns out and everything.

Rey remembers when Kenny was assigned to his unit. *Oh man, I got this meathead*, he thought. But he was genuine. Loyal. Rey didn't feel such loyalty from everyone. He felt Kenny would kill and die for him. He had no pretenses. Kenny only cared about what was in front of him. Ask him what he thought of Iraq, he'd probably say, I don't know. It would not have occurred to him to think about it one way or the other. He had not felt obligated to be nice to Iraqis, but he also had not felt obligated to be an asshole. Kenny was straight-up. What you saw was what you got.

Thing is, Kenny says, I wasn't going to my probation officer.

'Cause you're a meathead, Rick says.

I'll tell the prosecutor I was your team leader in Iraq, Rey says.

Make sure you get ahold of my girlfriend, Amber. She'll be tripping.

Kind of miss you, dawg, Rick says.

Miss you too. Thanks for coming.

I'll make calls, Rey says.

In the evening Rey packs his bag for the drive to Rochelle, Illinois. Rural highways to Interstates 44 and 55. He won't accomplish anything in Branson with Kenny in jail. He worries that prison could become a comfortable place for Kenny.

Prisoners, marines. They both live by rules different from

those of the civilian world. People tell Rey, With your experience you should become a cop. They don't get it. Marines were not in Iraq to protect and serve. Marines were there to kill and destroy. Lucky for Iraq, his unit was not sent into Baghdad. Imagine, a bunch of Fallujah guys storming the capital. Would have burned it down. All right, bitches, we got this.

Glad you're back; we prayed for you, friends and family told Rey when he returned from Iraq. He wanted to know, What about the four thousand-plus guys who died? What about Levi and Kenny, who made it back but are struggling? Their families didn't pray for them?

Some things about the war Rey has not told his family. Like the time Corporal Miska wasted a barking dog before it gave away their position. Then he shot its puppies. It boiled down to this: a dog opening them up to a possible ambush, or just smoking it and its puppies too. Because the puppies would die anyway. How do you explain that kind of compassion to a civilian?

One marine flipped out in Fallujah. Just sat in his Humvee like a mule. Get the fuck off the Humvee. No. He wouldn't move. He was done. Checked out. Shaking. He was sent back in the next day with Yeager and Gonzo and hit a house. Gonzo got shot in the arm, another marine shot in the throat. Yeager shot the insurgent. The wigged-out marine fell down the stairs and ran out. He was sent to Bahria, Rey thinks.

The marines kept a skull in one house. Set it on a shelf. No bottom jaw. A hole in the right temple. The Iraqi army showed up and saw it. No, mister, they told the marines. Like it was voodoo shit. They threw it in the courtyard. *Plunk*, like a watermelon. Then it started to smell. Stuff was still inside it.

Sometimes it occurred to them they were playing around with someone's head.

At the start of the Fallujah campaign, Rey remembers approaching one house and feeling the walk sink below his feet. He was still a private first class and ordered to dig. Maybe it was a weapons cache. He uncovered a duffel bag. Dude probably had money, someone said. Maybe Woodbury or Norton. He yanked on the handle and the bag opened. A body wrapped in a blanket. The smell. Rey had never smelled anything like that before. They left it and moved on to the next house. Dogs probably ate it.

Kurt Poliska, 28, Rochelle, Illinois
Iraq deployment:
January 2006–July 2006

Every once in a while do you get that dream? Kurt asks Rey. That dream of, Where's my rifle? One time, Kurt dreamed he was in a firefight and dropped his rifle. *Oh shit*, he thought in his dream.

When he returned home he started applying for jobs like crazy. Security jobs. Got a lot of interviews. He was told, We wanted to see you because we just didn't believe your résumé. Twenty-three years old, and you say you were on security detail at Camp David? And then you served in Iraq? Amazing, but we need someone with more work experience. Oh, and thank you for your service.

A lot of the time, Kurt hung out. When he didn't watch TV, he lay on the floor. What am I going to do today? It pissed him off. He had heard about tax breaks for companies that hired vets. Hire me and save money. But no one did. He enrolled at

Northern Illinois University and then transferred to Western Illinois University to major in emergency management. He hopes to complete his degree soon.

Did I just waste four years of my life in the Marines? he asks Rey. All the high school kids he knew growing up have graduated from college, and here he was at twenty-eight, attending classes with eighteen-year-olds. A grown-ass man. He had commanded marines, moved millions of dollars of equipment.

Saddam was a bad dude, no doubt. But after a while, Kurt realized he was not fighting Saddam's regime but some other group of guys who had decided to pick a fight with the Americans. He would have preferred going to Afghanistan. Something more in line with the War on Terror.

You look at the Arab Spring, at Egypt, what if it would have happened organically in Iraq without us? Rey says.

It could have happened, Kurt says.

It could have not.

What if crickets had machine guns? Birds wouldn't fuck with them.

After he got out, Kurt felt guilty about guys still in Iraq being blown up while he was trying to figure out what to do with his life. He's glad the U.S. ended the war. Glad for everyone who made it home. He doesn't know if ending the war was good for Iraq, but at this point, he doesn't give a shit. He did expect more news coverage.

Kurt has heard about a few of the guys. Hawley is studying international relations; Miska is in the National Guard. Pioske had a kid. Rensi attends Bible school.

He hasn't thought of Cayer in the longest time. Kurt picked on him too, but not nearly as bad as other guys. One sergeant jumped down Cayer's throat for not wearing a T-shirt. No one else was wearing a T-shirt.

Kurt expected culture shock when he returned home. All of a sudden he was sitting on a bus, heading back to Camp Pendleton. Holy shit, he was in California. He remembers California as being really clean compared to Iraq and its mountains of trash on most roads. That surprised him more than anything.

Kurt doesn't have flashbacks, or whatever it is people say combat veterans always have. Sometimes he gets irritated with friends who complain about their jobs. Your job doesn't suck, dude, Kurt tells them. On a scale of suck, you're only a number two.

He thinks he may have come closer to dying at home than he did in Iraq. On February 14, 2008, a gunman entered a Northern Illinois University auditorium where Kurt was attending an oceanography class. It was a Tuesday–Thursday class, 2:00–3:15 p.m. The professor was talking about some sludge in a tidal zone. Fifteen minutes to go, and in walks this dude. Kurt noticed a shotgun down his left side, then saw him raise it. He reverted to his military training, dropped to one knee, and took cover behind the back of a chair. He remembers thinking, This is only a quarter inch of plastic.

He saw a girl frozen in her chair, reached for her hoodie, but instead grabbed her by the hair and yanked her to the floor.

He saw the gunman reloading his pistol. He knew that took time. He's reloading! he shouted to a girl crawling on the floor. Go! Get up! she screamed to the students behind her, and they bolted through the doors.

Later, while he was being debriefed, a police officer told Kurt he did not seem that upset. To tell you the truth, sir, Kurt said, it's not the first time someone has shot at me.

The gunman killed six students before killing himself. Kurt wonders if he could have done more.

You didn't have a weapon, Rey reminds him. No Kevlar. No backup.

Still, Kurt says.

Rey crosses the Illinois border into Iowa on Highway 20. He has never seen a state so flat as Iowa. The broad, silent farm fields, isolated houses. No trees. Rey looks forward to seeing Topete. Topete was with him in Fallujah the day after Rey's unit lost five marines.

On December 12, 2004, Corporal Ian Stewart with the Third Battalion, Fifth Marines, Kilo Company, ran to the second floor of a house without waiting for backup. Insurgents opened up on him. For about an hour heavy fighting ensued. Stewart had died by the time the marines reached him.

A sergeant told Rey to enter the next house and work his way to the roof. Gunfire split open a marine's cheek, and he collapsed into Rey's arms. Then another marine ran from the house, pale as a ghost. Staff Sergeant Melvin L. Blazer Jr., thirty-eight, he said, was in the house and had been shot in the stairwell. Who's there with him? Rey yelled. He pulled some guys together to get Blazer, shouting, Get your shit up there! *You* get up there! another marine yelled back. He did. He saw Blazer on the floor, stood over his body, and fired into the rooms at the insurgents shooting at him. He told a marine who had been pinned by enemy fire behind a wall to go under his fire and get Blazer. He started walking backward as the marine dragged Blazer's body.

Then Blazer's weapon caught on the stairwell. Another marine unhooked it and left it. When Rey reached the first floor, someone said Blazer's weapon was still upstairs. They could not leave it for the enemy. Rey ran back and got it. Everything so loud his ears stopped registering the noise. He was freaked. Not pissing and shitting himself, but amped. A Lance Corporal Norton grabbed him. Just stand behind this Humvee and wait, Norton said. Norton had a kind of calm that helped clear Rey's head. He was a hell of a shooter too. Killed an insurgent firing from a moving Humvee into a moving Toyota Tercel. Got a commendation. Hey, you killed somebody. Job well done.

For his actions, Rey received a commendation too, the Bronze Star. But he wasn't thinking of medals as he tried to sleep that night. He lay on the floor of a school, shaking. He didn't know if it was from the cold or coming down from all the adrenaline. There was no time to take a week off to mourn. A memorial would be held at the end of his deployment in Iraq and another one stateside.

At Camp Pendleton, Rey told Blazer's wife what had happened. He saw his children, a girl and a boy. He had seen the boy before, when he was first deployed. The boy was dressed in child-size desert cammies. Rey thought of the boy when he first saw Blazer's body. Despite the noise and shouting and smoke and the gun in his hand, he could still see him hugging his father goodbye.

Apolonio "Polo" Topete, 27, Sioux Center, Iowa
Iraq deployments:
June 2003–September 2003
September 2004–April 2005
January 2006–August 2006

Polo remembers the weather. Middle of summer, 128 degrees. He had just landed on his first deployment. Second day, and guys are passing out from dehydration. Al Diwaniyah, south of Baghdad, middle of nowhere. Water got so hot it was like drinking out of a microwave. Rifles hot. Pistol grip was rubber, but the barrel, oh fuck. Toward the end of the deployment they got some ice. Seems they always got stuff at the end of a deployment.

They could patrol with no Kevlar on then. Summer 2003. The people liked them. Iraq was nice. Sometimes nothing went on. Sometimes you woke up just to tell yourself you had one day less on your deployment. I'm a quarter of the way there, you might say. I'm a couple months out from going home.

People would ask Polo, How many people you kill? He would toss out a random number. Ten. I killed ten.

Really?

Shut the fuck up, he would tell them.

Other times he tried to explain it. Combat's different, he would say. It's like you're hunting and being hunted. They would never know that feeling. Being there, being around marines. That sense of someone you can't see looking at you and trying to kill you. Hear the *zing*. That was close.

A lot goes through your mind. Is this where I die? It's not. Fuck. On to the next day. Here I go again. Is this it? Like that time he, Fredenburg, and another marine were on an elevated road by a canal. A cliff rose nearby, overlooking a little grassy area. Fredenburg was sitting. Two rounds pop the dirt in front of him. Where was it coming from? They all started running. Funny now, because no one was hurt.

Do you think you could have stayed in? Rey asks.

Yeah, it does cross my mind, Polo says. You never know what might happen. I miss it, miss everyone. I'd re-up if everyone else did. I wouldn't feel safe with a bunch of different guys. I'd get to know them, but it wouldn't be the same.

You showed up in Fallujah on December 13, Rey says. I saw you and Gaudy. That was the day Anderson got hit. Gibson was pissed; Anderson was his buddy.

Then we had to go back to patrol in the middle of the city, Polo says. To inventory stuff of the guys who'd been hurt, wounded in action, killed. Hawley, Cisneros, me. Jackets, weapons, to make sure we had everyone's stuff. I remember Sergeant Kirk's jacket. It had blood on it. Not a lot. We lost him.

When Cayer died, Polo thought he was another marine killed in action. He heard his death announced on the radio and thought Cayer had been smoked by a sniper. Shot in the head. Polo did not factor in suicide. Guys were getting killed and Cayer did that to himself? He can understand war fucking someone up, but he thought Cayer acted selfishly taking his own life.

Polo had felt sorry for Cayer. Everyone gave him a hard time. He wore glasses, looked nerdy. A lot of guys gave him shit. They gave shit to each other too, but it was like brothers. Don't say that about my wife, I'm serious, a guy told Polo one time. Okay, Polo chilled. He didn't touch that subject anymore, but other guys did. If you showed it bugged you, everyone jumped on. Polo was given shit for liking Asian chicks. You like what? He doesn't like Asian chicks anymore. None out here in Sioux Center.

Seen anybody?

No, Polo says. We're all over the place.

After his discharge, he worked for a furniture manufacturer. The kind of place that makes stuff for clinics and hospitals. On the job, he used a nail gun. Every once in a while he'd fire it at nothing. *Pop, pop, pop.*

Now he earns $21 an hour at a bacon manufacturing plant. He recently married. When he thinks of Iraq, he remembers patrols and stuff. All the shit they did fucking up Fallujah. There was one house with a room filled with dishware. Polo and another guy threw plates. He supposes they were pissed and wanted to break shit. Just break fucking shit. That whole room. They fucked it all up.

Rey leaves Sioux Center, drives through uninhabited expanses. Leaves lots of time to think on the long drive home. Pete, Levi, Kenny, Kurt, Polo, Cayer, Rey. They had all been kids. They thought they were men doing men things, but they were kids.

Rey could return to Texas and stare at the ceiling like Levi and imagine different endings for Cayer and everyone else who died in Iraq, but nothing would change. The dead would remain dead. Rey understands this now, and the knowledge gives him some peace and allows him to sleep at night. But a lot of times he has to be good and tired for the questions not to wake him.

For the longest time, Rey felt Sergeant Blazer's death was unfair. He got blasted in a stairway trying to help other marines. What gave Rey the right to be alive? He thought that way for months until he realized that if Blazer had survived he would not be sitting on his ass. He would not let the world go by. He would do more than that. Rey has spoken with Blazer's son, Erik. Erik found Rey on Facebook and called him one day last year. I wanted to thank you, he said. Your father would have done the same for me, Rey told him. Erik was in high school and wanted to go to college and become a meteorologist. He was okay, he said. Rey thought, *Stay okay.*

Rey had gotten his war, but he had not thought it through to its logical conclusion. Men would die. He had not wanted men to die. Not on his watch. He had wanted everyone to come home. They came so close on his second deployment; then Cayer died.

Maybe had he not been so wrapped up about going home, Rey would have taken the time to speak with Cayer. He doesn't know. What if, what if, what if, what if? Say whatever you wanted about him, Cayer was still a person. A good kid. Maybe not a good marine, but a good kid. Had he lived, Cayer would be out of the Marine Corps today. Rey feels sure he would look back at some of his problems and realize they were nothing.

Pete, Levi, Kenny, Kurt, Polo, Cayer, Rey. Despite the uniform, each one different. They came from states all across the country, cut their hair and dressed the same, called each other by their last names and became friends. Yet the word "veteran" doesn't cover it. They aren't the guys in the recruiting posters.

Through the silence of an empty highway shrouded in winter chill, Rey wonders if the country understands that.